S0-BCI-890

Parenting in a Pandemic

How to help your family through COVID-19

Kelly Fradin, MD

Disclaimer: The material in this book is supplied for educational purposes only. I am a physician, but not your physician. No book can replace the personalized medical advice of a trusted physician. Please consult with your health care provider before making decisions regarding your child's health. Particularly if your child or family member suffers from chronic medical issues.

Copyright © 2020 Kelly Fradin MD

Adviceigivemyfriends.com

All rights reserved.

ISBN: 978-1-7355927-0-1

Cover design by Victoria Black

For all the parents struggling through this pandemic.

Contents

Prologue

A lot has been written about parental burnout during this strange time. Parents are overwhelmed and overextended. When the pandemic first hit and we thought of it as a few weeks at home, we all imagined we could muddle through. However, as it continues on, parents are dealing with unprecedented levels of stress.

We know a lot about just how unhealthy toxic stress is. Adverse childhood experiences — being the victim of abuse, witnessing violence, or having instability in your home — are known to be linked with lifelong health problems, from increasing the risk of diabetes and heart attacks to causing cancer and early death. [1]

Social isolation is known to worsen the effects of stress. Excess stress leads to anxiety, which causes worse sleep. Worse sleep leads to decreased capacity to handle stress, which leads to a vicious cycle. We have moved out of the concept of coronavirus as a two-week sprint and into the understanding that coping with coronavirus is a marathon. Every parent I talk to is worried. And there is no clear end in sight.

Sometimes, as a pediatrician, I increase a parent's stress when I bring a new problem to their attention. However, my favorite part of my job is when I can confidently and convincingly reassure a parent. Seeing the brow crease relax and hearing the sigh of relief make me feel as if I've done something to help.

During a pandemic, what can I help with? I am no help if you've lost your job or you're stressed about your household finances. However, as a pediatrician, I can help in other ways. I can help you think about the risk of coronavirus to your children, whether they are newborns, toddlers, school-age kids, or teens. I can help you put the risk to the adults in your life in context. I can give you tools to help you talk with your children about coronavirus in ways they can understand. I can help you think about how to make a decision to attend daycare or send your children to school. If you're worried about your children's social skills and academic development while they're stuck at home, I can share ideas to help. If your children are anxious or depressed, I can help you address this and consider when to ask for help. If you're fighting with your family about different isolation styles, I can give you some tools to help you navigate the sensitive and difficult conversations.

In short, I think I can help a lot if you'll let me.

As a pediatrician, it's my job to help families find their way. I am used to helping counsel parents on making decisions. Decisions during a pandemic are no different. I felt my calling toward medicine at an early age. As a preschooler, I declared my intention to be a doctor.

Compared to most enthusiastic little ones, I had more exposure to the health care profession. When I was three, I was diagnosed with bilateral Wilms Tumor, a rare kidney cancer. My parents sought treatment at a first-rate institution, and I made a complete recovery after chemotherapy, radiation, and surgeries. I was inspired by my physicians and the way they changed my life and I wanted to be just like them.

I also saw the toll my health problems took on my family. In many ways, my childhood cancer was harder on my mother than it was on me. The fear, the stress, the unknowns and inability to plan all haunted my mother as she navigated that time and for years following. In some ways, this experience is universal when it comes to facing a serious health threat. The disease is like a rock that hits a pond and sinks to the bottom, but the ripples cause secondary impacts we can't always predict or understand. Surviving a health scare and watching my family navigate the difficult time surrounding it give me insights into what it's like to be sick or struggle through.

Perhaps because of this perspective on medicine, I knew entering college that my science classes would only take me so far in my medical career. I chose to major in psychology and learn more about the human mind, how we make decisions and how we think. I wrote my undergraduate thesis on the biophysiological response to stress, looking at student responses to stress. These years studying stress and resilience are relevant now because they provide a rich background for me as I approach helping your family through this pandemic.

I ended up pursuing pediatrics because I love the variety — a newborn and adolescent require entirely different skill sets and knowledge bases. While sometimes primary care doctors are said to know a little about a lot, I try my best to read broadly and know a lot about a lot. I also love pediatrics because children come with their own built-in support team — their families.

During my residency, I did some extra research in Kawasaki disease and the impact of multiple viruses on children hospitalized with respiratory illnesses. After residency, I spent a few years as an attending physician at a complex care practice at an academic children's hospital. There I worked with children with medical complexity — survivors of congenital heart disease or extreme prematurity and children with complex genetic or developmental impairments. Getting to know their families in such an intimate way, often seeing them for four to six visits a year plus one or two hospital stays, helped me learn the various ways families cope in a crisis and learn what supports are the most useful.

After I had my children, I took a more manageable job working in school health. Here I spent my days thinking about population health and understanding the role schools play in promoting children's well-being.

My journey at times has taken me in directions I wouldn't have predicted. But now, during this pandemic, I think back and remember how each step in my career path has prepared me to help others now. I spent time learning more about stress, mental health, respiratory viruses, Kawasaki disease, and public health than most pediatricians. And maybe it's for a reason. I hope that these experiences have prepared me to help you navigate this time.

The nature of a pandemic is that we learn as we go. Since this guide is targeted at parents, while I will review our current understanding of the scientific studies, I will focus on coping with the stress and making decisions. These approaches should not change even if the science does.

Hopefully vaccines will emerge and I will need to be revise this book. But hopefully this is somewhere to start and a resource to help now.

To stay up to date as the news unfolds, please subscribe to my newsletter via my website, adviceigivemyfriends.com. I promise to send any important updates out as they occur. And remember that your primary care doctor and your child's pediatrician are your allies and best resources as you consider how to get through this pandemic.

Coronavirus Basics

What is COVID-19?

As the pandemic evolves, sometimes we lose sight of fundamental facts that are helpful. Coronaviruses are not new. Coronaviruses were discovered in the 1960s and are one of the most common causes of colds, accounting for 20-30%. The name coronavirus comes from the way each individual virus looks under electron microscopy, with a halo similar to the corona of the sun.

Specifically bad strains of coronaviruses have caused epidemics before — Middle Eastern Respiratory Syndrome (MERS) and Sudden Acute Respiratory Syndrome (SARS). This is why some vaccine efforts aren't starting from scratch. These viruses stopped spreading before vaccine development could be completed. Subsequent funding and prioritization of vaccine efforts waned. But communities closer to where MERS and SARS hit were more prepared for containment efforts.

From a parenting perspective, I don't think it's worthwhile to spend too much time considering where the virus originated. This strain, SARS-CoV-2, or COVID-19, is different from coronaviruses that previously circulated every year. It's novel — most of us don't have protection based on prior illness, and we are still learning specifics about the virus.

The timeline of spread seems pretty settled — the virus began to spread in Wuhan, China, around November 2019. The spread started small clusters of infection in more and more places until it hit NYC hard in March 2020. From NYC it has now spread all over the US.

So let's talk about what we need to know as parents. While some of the following is pretty technical, I think it provides a helpful context for the more practical advice later in the book. But if you find it too dry, skip ahead; you can always refer back to it later on.

How does it spread?

I believe that news and major health organizations have vacillated too much on this topic. The evidence seems clear that the primary route of spread in the community is by droplet, so let's dig in to learn what that means.

In all hospitals, we consider which precautions are necessary to protect both patients and staff. Particularly in the winter in children's hospitals, we take great care to make sure children admitted after a surgery are not roomed with a child with an infectious reason for admission, like influenza. In a hospital setting, in accordance with the CDC recommendations,[2] we think of contact, droplet, and airborne transmission.

Infections spread by contact transmission can be either direct or indirect. A direct contact spread would be from an animal bite, touching someone with scabies, or touching a herpetic lesion. The pathogen jumps over and causes damage. Indirect contact occurs through an intermediate object. If a doctor doesn't wash hands well, he or she may carry pathogens — such as the bacteria that cause skin infections or infectious diarrhea — from one patient to the next.

Droplet transmission is a variant of contact transmission, as most illnesses spread by infected droplets can also be spread by direct or indirect contact. Respiratory droplets are emitted when someone who is infected coughs, sneezes, or talks and can carry the pathogen to the respiratory tract or mucous membrane (i.e. eyes, nose, mouth) of others near them. Lots of common infections are transmitted this way — for example, pertussis (whooping cough), influenza, rhinovirus, and strep throat. To protect yourself from droplets, distance and regular surgical masks are effective, particularly when coupled with hand hygiene.

Other illnesses, like measles, chicken pox, and tuberculosis, are "airborne." That means tiny droplet residue can survive and remain in the air for longer periods of time. Air currents may lead to infection even in those who have not had face-to-face contact with an individual infected with one of these pathogens. Airborne precautions require more serious interventions — typically rooms with special ventilation systems in the hospital to prevent spread. N-95 masks, which trap smaller particles than the surgical mask, are necessary for healthcare personnel exposed to these infections.

COVID-19 seems to be a hybrid. In typical settings outside a hospital or clinic, infected individuals produce droplets — as many as a thousand a minute while speaking loudly without a mask.[3] The infectious dose of COVID-19 — how many viral particles are required to get sick — is unknown but is estimated to be between 750 and 1,000, similar to that of the flu and other coronaviruses.[4] However, in some situations, such as when inserting a breathing tube or doing a deep swab of the nose, some of the virus may be aerosolized and persist in the air for longer periods of time. It seems likely that activities like singing or shouting may increase the risk of generating aerosols.

This is important as we make plans to protect ourselves. Masks and hand hygiene are the cornerstones of decreasing risk of transmission. Adequate ventilation is likely to be protective, too.

What are the symptoms?

As a parent, the symptoms and signs of coronavirus infection are the most important thing to know. If someone in your family has these, it's time to contact your doctor to consider testing. We're still learning about COVID-19, but the consensus is that the most common symptoms include the following.[5,6]

COVID-19 Symptom	Frequency in kids	Frequency in adults
Fever	42 - 56% >99.5F or >37.5C	36 - 45% >100.4F or >38C
Cough	44 - 54%	34 - 55%
Shortness of breath	11 - 13%	26 - 31%
Muscle aches	34 - 37%	10 - 45%
Headache	4 - 27%	5 - 46%
Loss of taste or smell	7 - 9%	1 - 13%
Sore throat	4 - 24%	5 - 28%
Congestion or runny nose	7 - 22%	2 - 9%
Nausea or vomiting	~ 10%	5 - 13%
Diarrhea	9 - 13%	8 - 22%

Because of limitations in testing early on, it's important to emphasize these percentages are out of people who are sick and seek care for symptoms of coronavirus. Since we know many children and adults have no symptoms, we shouldn't assume, for example, that 11% of children who have coronavirus have shortness of breath. Since we know that ~80% of children with coronavirus show no symptoms, it's more accurate to estimate that 11% *of the 20% who have symptoms* have shortness of breath. This means that only approximately 2% of all children who test positive for coronavirus have shortness of breath.

Symptoms vary considerably by age. Fever and cough are not always present, even among those with symptoms of coronavirus. Muscle aches, headaches, sore throat, and diarrhea are frequent symptoms.

Life post-coronavirus should include a high *index of suspicion*. Index of suspicion is a medical term that refers to our initial impression of the likelihood of the disease. We should assume that most symptoms during this time of a pandemic may be related to coronavirus. If you don't feel well or when your children don't feel well, consider pursuing testing and reaching a diagnosis.

How is it diagnosed?

Original studies in China before a test was developed used CT scans to look for damaged lung tissue. Now we use nasal swabs or saliva samples to look for detectable virus, using a technique called nucleic acid amplification (NAA). The code for the viral protein is converted; then, using Polymerase Chain Reaction techniques (PCR), the code is multiplied to facilitate detection. Nucleic acid amplification tests are very good tests, both at identifying truly positive specimens and excluding negative specimens without the virus.

Two of the biggest limitations to the test are unavoidable no matter how good the test is. First, given the natural progression of the virus, there may not be detectable virus in an obtained specimen early on. The incubation period — the time between being exposed to the virus and falling sick — is about five days but may be as long as 14 days. In the pre-symptomatic stage, the day or two before you start feeling crummy, you may be transmitting the virus even though you are not showing symptoms. Even if sick, you may test negative for the first two days of feeling ill — despite being potentially contagious. All of this is to say, if you get tested one day after exposure and the test is negative, that doesn't tell you if you will get or transmit coronavirus.

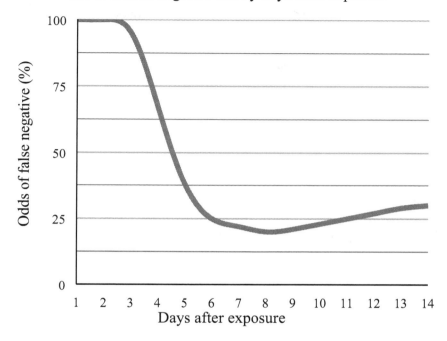

Odds of a false negative test by days after exposure

This chart follows the likely testing results of someone exposed to COVID-19 who will fall sick. As you can see testing the first 2 days after exposure is not helpful, you'll test negative nearly 100% of the time. Even testing the day you start feeling ill (on average day 5) will miss 38% of people. Testing 3 days after symptoms begin or on day 8, has the best odds of correctly identifying a positive case. On day 8 you'll identify 80% of the cases.[7]

Second, the specimen is getting the test, not the entire person. My best analogy for this is strep throat. Getting a very good specimen where my cotton swab rubs all the right spots for long enough with a squirming, crying, sick child is often very difficult. The specimen matters a lot. If I tap your nose with the brush, I'll obtain a specimen with very different levels of virus than if I had dug in the back of your nasopharynx. As uncomfortable as a good nasopharyngeal specimen is to obtain, it's essential.

Other tests for active infection are being developed. Antigen tests are rapid and results are often available in less than an hour. These tests detect tiny bits of virus in the specimen. Positive antigen tests are pretty reliable at correctly identifying specimens with virus in them. The rapid point-of-care tests enabled with this technology can be very helpful for controlling spread of disease.

If you have symptoms and use an NAA test, depending on where you live, you may wait up to a week for results. This wait time also impacts all the people you may have exposed who may change their behavior — pursue testing or isolate — as a result of your potentially positive tests. However, negative results from an antigen test can't be trusted as much as the NAA tests because they skip the amplification step. So when you really have to be confident in negative results, the best test is the somewhat slower NAA.

What is an antibody?

Part of having a plan for moving past this pandemic depends on our understanding of herd immunity and individual immunity.

The estimate is that around 70% of the population needs to be immune to coronavirus to stop the pandemic. This is because each person who is immune to coronavirus won't contribute to its spread, so they effectively become dead ends for the virus. If there are enough dead ends, for each sick person, fewer new people get sick and eventually the spread of the virus stops.

This doesn't mean the virus disappears. People can still transmit it, particularly in groups who haven't been exposed.

So, how do we know if someone is immune? This is a surprisingly difficult question. Our immune system is extraordinarily complex. The most widely known and discussed part of the immune system is our humoral immunity — essentially, the antibody circulating in our blood. Antibodies are large Y-shaped proteins that bind to the pathogen (i.e., virus or bacteria) and flag it for destruction.

Every person has a unique and specific response to a pathogen. Antibodies have a three-dimensional shape. Some antibodies might be the perfect fit and capture every single copy of the pathogen. Others may be too loose or too tight and demonstrate worse avidity or propensity to capture the virus. Laboratories can develop tests to examine the avidity, but these tests are not often used outside of research. The available COVID-19 antibody tests will report qualitative (yes or no antibodies) and quantitative (how many antibodies are in a milliliter of your blood) information.

So, how much antibody do you need per drop of blood to functionally defeat the intruding virus? This is mostly an educated guess. To know the answer to this definitively would require exposing volunteers to infections, which isn't ethical. Even if you have a high quantity of a good quality antibody, this may change over time.

Even if you have recovered from infection and have a good quality antibody with high quantity, studies have shown it may decrease over time. While the studies available thus far are small, they suggest that 40% of individuals who test positive after asymptomatic or mild coronavirus will lose antibodies within three months. Similarly, 13% of individuals who tested positive and were sick with coronavirus infection lost their measurable antibody.[8] This is common with other infections as well.

While this may be disappointing, it doesn't tell us what would happen if these people (i.e., those who had documented COVID-19 antibodies go away) were exposed to coronavirus infection again. Their bodies might rise to the challenge and produce antibodies on demand, thanks to cells called memory b-cells. And to make it more complicated, another category of immunity might defeat the intruder.

We have cell-mediated immunity in addition to antibody mediated or humoral immunity. These other immune cells are called t-cells because they are developed in the thymus. T-cells help regulate the innate immune system that controls the cytokines you may have heard about and directly kills infected cells. Individuals who have t-cells that can recognize coronavirus may be immune — we just don't know yet. I hope our understanding of this advances soon because, as we look at antibody prevalence as a marker to see where we are on the march toward herd immunity, without better understanding of cell-mediated immunity, we'll have an unclear picture of our protection.

Putting aside our concerns about community health, should your family get antibody tested? If you've lived in an area that's had extensive community transmission or you've had an illness you struggled through at home similar to coronavirus, you can consider it. Your body needs at least 2 weeks and more likely 4-6 to test positive for antibodies after an infection. If you have a higher likelihood of having had coronavirus, you may show antibodies.

The biggest question is whether you should change your behavior based on the results. If we don't know antibodies will protect you from reinfection or transmitting the disease, you shouldn't change your behavior based on the results. But knowing you have antibodies may help you have peace of mind. You can think of it as one layer in the plans to protect your family, but alone I wouldn't count on it. The likelihood that the antibody test is a false positive — that it indicates you have antibodies to a virus you haven't been exposed to — is low, but certainly it's possible.

The larger flaw in the antibody test is that you test negative and you had the disease. Either your antibodies could fall below the cutoff for sufficient or your antibodies could have waned in your bloodstream and are now nearly undetectable. In this situation, you may be falsely worried by your lack of antibodies. As a physician, I'd rather you assume you are vulnerable to illness and protect yourself than have you think you are protected and fall sick again (or infect someone else).

It's a complex decision and luckily you aren't alone in making it. Your health care provider can walk you through the pros and cons and help you interpret any test results. But hopefully this background is helpful as you consider seeking testing.

Now that we've covered the coronavirus basics, let's dig into talking more about kids.

Coronavirus & Kids

What is the risk of coronavirus for most kids?

Any parent has an innate urge to protect their child. It's evolutionary. If we didn't, our species would not have survived. However, to appropriately make decisions to protect your child, you need a lot of information.

First you need to understand the maxgnitude of all the potential risks specific to you and your family. Sometimes we get very used to things and assume they are safe. Driving, for example — most people do it daily, but it is dangerous. Motor vehicle crashes are in the top three causes of deaths in the United States and the No. 1 cause of disability. Yet people are much more likely to worry about being injured by a crime than a car accident. And despite the well-known and described risks of the flu, most adults choose not to be vaccinated.[9]

We have to dive into the risk for severe disease and death from coronavirus so that we can understand our choices. While no one likes to think about the worst-case scenario or children suffering, by considering these numbers and how low they are, I can reassure you that your kids will most likely be OK if they get sick. I can't promise the same for your elderly family members.

The risk of severe disease from coronavirus is significantly higher for adults than children. In data from China, the U.S., the UK, and Italy, kids represent 20% of the population, approximately 2% of documented coronavirus cases, and less than 0.2% of the deaths.

Now, certainly this data isn't perfect. The 2% number refers to the percentage of positive test results from children. If our propensity to obtain testing were the same at every age, this number would be reliable, but it's not. Early on, we reserved testing for people requiring hospital care because we did not have enough protective apparel, swabs, or test kits for everyone who needed a test. Even now, there are still limitations in access to testing, and we know that sicker people are more likely to be tested. With more thoughtful sampling of children, we know that many more children have had coronavirus. As many as 80% of children who test positive for coronavirus may have no symptoms.[10]

Another problem in understanding how children have done with coronavirus is that we have profoundly changed our behavior to protect kids. Closing schools, keeping our distance, and staying home have reduced children's exposure. Data from March to May 2020 on whether children in the U.S. catch and transmit coronavirus show that adults drive spread. But during that time, most schools and daycares were closed and children were kept home.

To get around this behavior obstacle, we can try to understand risk of catching coronavirus and suffering from coronavirus by looking at early data from places that didn't have a chance to change behavior. Additionally, we can try to interpret data from places that have reopened early, though comparing different countries and even different states can be challenging. Variance exists between populations in obesity rates, education levels, mask compliance rates, density of living environments, and access to health care, so findings from other places may not translate perfectly into our own communities.

But, putting the numbers aside for a moment, we can discuss what happened to my colleagues at the Children's Hospital at Montefiore (CHAM) in the Bronx, NY, during the surge in the spring of 2020. CHAM consists of a pediatric emergency room and four inpatient floors and runs pretty close to full capacity. Early in the pandemic, the pediatric ER was restaffed for adult use. Three hospital floors were open to patients up to age 30, when normally the cutoff is 21. Then, a week or two later, adults took over one floor and half of the intensive care unit. So, children normally fill five floors of hospital, but adults were allowed on all but one and a half floors, and there was still enough space for children sick with coronavirus. During this time, the adult hospital census for coronavirus exploded from zero to over 1,832 — 150 of whom were cared for in the children's hospital without running out of space.[11] This is enormously reassuring.

To look more closely at the children hospitalized with coronavirus requires sophisticated understanding of how clinical studies work. With a quick read, the first report from the CDC on children and coronavirus implied that the rate of hospitalization was between 6% and 20%, nearly as high as adults. But that isn't the case at all, and it's essential to take a closer look.

These doctors looked at children who came to the hospital because they were quite sick, received testing, and subsequently were hospitalized. So these children are some of the 20% of children who have symptoms when sick (remember that 80% have no symptoms). So even if there is a 6% chance of requiring hospitalization in this group, if your child becomes sick with coronavirus at home, the risk of requiring hospitalization is closer to 6 out of 500, or 1.2%.

But wait: The risk is actually even lower than this for most kids. In groups of children who get hospitalized, many have risk factors for infection, including lung disease, heart disease, and immunosuppression. The largest case series to date showed that 77% of children hospitalized had underlying conditions[12]. Assuming your child is relatively healthy and falls outside of this group, the risk of hospitalization from coronavirus is 0.3%.

Furthermore, of children hospitalized for coronavirus, as many as half have another infection at the same time[13] — whether it was strep, the flu, RSV, or another respiratory virus. So, assuming your child only has one, that would bring the risk of hospitalization down even further.

Even among this small group of children with coronavirus who did need intensive medical care during the pandemic, most recovered fully. Sadly, some did not.

Looking at rates of child deaths from coronavirus is a more reliable but still imperfect way to consider the risk from coronavirus. As a pediatrician and a mother, I know that every death is a tragedy. But the fact is that deaths from coronavirus in children are very rare. Most countries report that 0 to 0.2% of coronavirus deaths occur in children.

Without a doubt, among the 3.5 million (and rapidly climbing) identified cases of coronavirus in the U.S., many children are included. The CDC has looked at leftover blood from non-coronavirus-related blood draws in an attempt to estimate the true number of cases. The current estimates suggest there are between 6 and 24 times the number of reported cases. Or, as many as 35 million cases might have actually occurred as of July 2020.[14] To help us understand how many children may have actually had coronavirus, scientists have built models such as the one utilized by CovKids Project[15] that estimates that, as of July 13, 2020, 1.8 million children have had coronavirus and 66 — or 0.004% — have died. While it's possible or even likely that we are off on how many children have had coronavirus, given our incomplete testing strategy, it's unlikely that we have missed any deaths.

All of these deaths occurred in children who tested positive for coronavirus, but it's unclear if coronavirus was the causative factor in each death. Without a doubt, many deaths were due to coronavirus, but when reading the individual case series of the few reported pediatric deaths in the medical literature, some are questionable. For example, the four cases reported in Italy included two children with complex congenital heart disease who had preoperative complications and at some point tested positive for coronavirus, a child with a severe inherited metabolic disorder whose family elected palliative care, and an infant with rare and aggressive cancer who was on chemotherapy.[16] These deaths are tragedies, but it's not certain that coronavirus was the driving factor associated with the death in all cases. As a proxy, though coronavirus is not the same as the flu, in a typical year, we live our lives and as many as 150 children die in the U.S. of the flu despite vaccines being available (and underutilized).

I am a survivor of an incredibly rare childhood cancer. My mother would say that when your child is sick, it doesn't matter if it was a one in a million chance — they are sick. She's not wrong. For the sake of your own child's safety, it's worth avoiding infection. When I hear of coronavirus parties and the "let's get it over with" idea, I want to cry. This isn't a good idea, as it's taking an unnecessary risk — though small to your child's health — without a proven benefit, since there is no guarantee of immunity. Additionally, an infected child may spread disease to others who may be higher risk for complications.

Please remember that, while kids have done very well with coronavirus overall, it is possible for them to spread disease in our community and we have to consider how their activities put others in our community at risk (teachers, doctors, parents, grandparents, etc.).

What about MIS-C?

Another risk to consider in children is Multisystem Inflammatory Syndrome In Children (MIS-C), the mysterious condition landing some children in intensive care units. Of all the updates I anticipate making in this book, I hope I can update the name of this syndrome. Multisystem Inflammatory Syndrome in Children is both a mouthful and very nonspecific. What do parents need to know about this syndrome? Should it change the way you worry about your kids falling sick with coronavirus? Let's discuss.

What we've seen is children presenting to the hospital quite sick — high fever and severe illness involving at least two different systems in the body. This table describes the CDC criteria for diagnosis and highlights the most common symptoms. [17, 18]

Diagnostic criteria of MIS-C
Fever >100.4F or >38.0C for at least 1 day
Abnormal labwork consistent with inflammation
Current or prior infection with COVID-19 • up to 4 weeks prior • can be suspected illness or exposure without symptoms
No obvious alternative diagnosis
Severe illness affecting at least two organ systems

Reported symptoms by organ system

Cardiac (80%)
- Low blood pressure
- Fast heart rate (97%)
- Inflammation of the heart (53%)
- Chest pain (11%)

Hematologic (68 - 80%)
- Blood clot (1 - 7%)

Gastrointestinal (80 - 92%)
- Abdominal pain (61%)
- Vomiting (58%)
- Diarrhea (49%)

Respiratory (53-87%)
- Cough (31%)
- Shortness of breath (19%)

Skin (56 - 80%)
- Rash (60%)
- Red eyes (56%)
- Peeling and irritation of mouth (27 - 42%)

Extremities (8-42%)
- Muscle or joint pain (20%)
- Pain or swelling (9%)
- Lymphadenopathy (6%)

Renal / Kidney (3 - 13%)
- Decreased urine output

Neurologic (5 - 30%)
- Headache (29%)
- Confusion (2%)

Children with MIS-C were a median of 8.9 years old and were relatively evenly distributed between the three groups 0-5, 6-12, and 13-20 years of age. It's important to identify children with this promptly and seek care from an institution that has the specialists and intensive care unit to handle cases. This isn't available everywhere, and the CDC has a national provider line to discuss confusing cases and facilitate early referral to specialists who can help. If you think your child has symptoms of MIS-C, either get your pediatrician on the phone immediately or head to the closest emergency room.

Children with MIS-C look similar to kids with the well-established Kawasaki disease — a similar yet distinctly different illness. To simplify, you can think of both as conditions where the immune system responds to a viral trigger and goes into overdrive. The overactive immune system begins to cause significant inflammation all over the body. This inflammation can cause permanent damage. You may have heard of some adults with coronavirus suffering "cytokine storm." This is a little different, but the general principle is the same.

With Kawasaki Disease, common respiratory viruses — including adenovirus, enterovirus, rhinovirus, metapneumovirus and coronavirus — are thought to be triggers, although this isn't entirely understood. Coronavirus is almost certainly the trigger for MIS-C, given the time this syndrome came to light. Most but not all of the cases either tested positive for active coronavirus (i.e., nose swab detected virus) or antibodies to coronavirus (suggesting recovery from COVID-19). While the severity and unknowns of MIS-C warrant attention, so far the condition seems both very rare and very treatable.

The risk of MIS-C is unknown because we do not know precisely how many children have had COVID-19. Not only do testing shortages persist, but also children are undersampled due to the fact that they often have asymptomatic or mild disease. We can estimate, though, that at the peak of coronavirus in NYC, hundreds of thousands of children had COVID-19. Using rough numbers, we know there are about 2 million children in NYC and we estimate that as many as 15% had coronavirus prior to MIS-C emerging. This means about 200,000 children with coronavirus resulted in 99 cases of MIS-C. These numbers would indicate 0.05% of children with COVID-19 developed MIS-C or, more reassuringly, 99.95% of children did not. Early data from Florida and Detroit indicate these estimates are in the correct range.

This back-of-the-envelope guess about the risk of MIS-C is limited — certainly it could be off. Maybe cases have been missed, although, given the severity of presenting symptoms, I think it's unlikely the case count is much higher. Or perhaps the 99 should be lower because it includes some children who had Kawasaki instead of MIS-C and had a different viral trigger, but also had coronavirus. No one knows. But I think it's helpful as a parent, because it does give us a sense of the magnitude of the risk. The real number may be different, but any way you slice it, MIS-C is a very rare complication.

The other consideration is how these children do. Several children have died of MIS-C. Children with MIS-C require supportive care in the intensive care unit with assistance with their blood pressure and sometimes help breathing. Treatments including intravenous immunoglobulin and aspirin to calm the immune response have been used successfully. Most children affected with MIS-C have required up to a week in the hospital but have appeared to make a full recovery with no anticipated long-term issues.

The manifestation of MIS-C in the heart are most worrisome. Case series have shown that 9% have aneurysms or dilations of the blood vessels supplying the heart. We've also seen high rates of myocarditis (53%) or inflammation of the heart muscle, heart muscle dysfunction (38%) and arrhythmia (12%). Without waiting to see what the echocardiograms show in six months, we simply don't know how these kids will do going forward. But the fact that most are able to be discharged quickly after being so sick makes me optimistic that we'll see good recovery in the children who received proper treatment.

As a community and public health-oriented pediatrician, I am worried about missed cases of MIS-C. During the peak of the pandemic in NYC, the hospitals were so overwhelmed the clear message was to stay home at all costs. In normal times, no parent would attempt to keep children home with the severity of symptoms associated with MIS-C. However, I do think it's possible that, during peak pandemic in NYC, we may have missed cases. This matters because, if you really think your child had this and they were really very sick and stayed home, I would contact your pediatrician to discuss whether a cardiac evaluation is needed.

As a parent, I am not worried about MIS-C! I know that if my children have this very rare complication and I seek prompt care likely, they will make a full recovery. I also know that very rare complications like this exist with other viruses, too, such as Guillain Barre (an autoimmune damage to the peripheral nervous system that can cause weakness following viral infection). When things are so severe and make the news, it can be quite disturbing to parents, but I'd argue something this rare and mostly treatable shouldn't drive your decision-making.

Long-term issues after primary coronavirus infection

Some articles in the media have insinuated that children may suffer long-term issues after coronavirus. This amorphous serious risk really worries many parents. COVID-19 is novel, we are still learning a lot about it, and no one can be certain. We want to cast a broad net and imagine all the things we may be missing and all the ways in which coronavirus could harm our children. I have heard from a lot of parents with these worries. "I was planning to send my kids to school, but then I heard coronavirus could cause long-term disability." As a pediatrician, I am not worried about the direct long-term effects of coronavirus for children.

Before diving into why, I want to state my goal in reassuring you is not to diminish the true urgency of containing coronavirus. As of August 14th 2020, nearly 170,000 people have died of coronavirus in the United States. While most of these are adults, 104 children have died. Masking, social distancing, and taking precautions to limit the spread of coronavirus are essential to protect our families and our larger community.

But it pains me to hear already over-stretched and over-stressed parents panicked about something that I do not consider a real threat. So let's discuss what has been published regarding long-term problems following coronavirus.

The Morbidity and Mortality Weekly report from the CDC published the results of a telephone survey that showed 20% of young adults experienced fatigue, cough, congestion and other symptoms 2-3 weeks after testing positive for coronavirus.[19] This finding is in the range of what we see following many other respiratory infections where symptoms like cough and fatigue can persist for up to two months. Further what's not emphasized is the likelihood that some of the individuals feeling better may have not elected to complete the survey so individuals with longer courses of symptoms may have been over-represented.

Similarly a study in Italy found that 87% of adults had persistent COVID-19 symptoms two weeks following discharge from the hospital.[20] Another study highlighted that 55% of adults hospitalized for more than two weeks for coronavirus experienced neurologic problems even 3 months after infection[21]. These articles highlight real and significant concerns for adults, particularly those unlucky enough to have severe coronavirus requiring hospitalization. A two-week hospitalization for any reason reflects a truly major medical illness and will require substantial recovery. We track hospitalizations because they are undesirable outcomes and this further describes what we already know.

This research should be done and discussed because doctors have to be prepared to meet the needs of these patients as they recover including increased demands for COVID-specific follow up clinics and rehabilitation. But these studies don't change the fact that most children who catch coronavirus are asymptomatic and do quite well.

COVID-19 is new. We do not have long-term follow up data to guide us, but we do have some clues. The CovKids Project estimates that 2.6 million children have already had coronavirus in the US alone. Internationally it's another order of magnitude. Enough children have had COVID-19 for long enough that we have been able to identify the multi-system inflammatory syndrome (MIS-C) which is estimated to affect as many as 3 out of 10,000 children after infection.

So certainly we have not detected every possible issue, and we'll have to continue studying children who present with unexpected issues. But it's unlikely that we haven't noticed a common problem. Most viral complications begin soon after infection so we should have detected surges in most complications by now. We know that almost all viruses have rare sequelae, every year people suffer from Guillain Barré Syndrome, Kawasaki Disease, transverse myelitis, myalgic encephalitis / chronic fatigue syndrome and other illnesses. Most parents haven't heard of these terrible complications for a reason - they are extraordinarily rare.

Coronavirus has shown a propensity to cause vascular inflammation and heart damage in adults with severe infection requiring hospitalization, but we haven't seen this in other groups and it seems unlikely that mild cases of coronavirus have any long-term heart issues. The heart damage induced by MIS-C has so far appeared to respond well to treatment.

Early in the pandemic, physicians in China used CT scans of the lungs to make a diagnosis of coronavirus. These showed some children with mild disease had changes in the lungs. CT scan is very sensitive to detect lung problems, frequently a child who has abdominal CT has unrelated issues noted in the bottom of the lungs. We haven't yet heard whether these changes persist, but respiratory syncytial virus (RSV), a common respiratory infection in children, is known to cause damage to the lungs when children have it at a young age. Having RSV before age 2 can increase the risk of reactive airways or asthma that requires treatment. However we do see that as children's lungs continue to grow until age 8, this damage is almost always outgrown. Could coronavirus cause something similar? Yes, but we have no reason to think that it would be more serious.

So what do I worry about with our children and coronavirus - mental health. Loneliness, screens, and disruption of our lives can all increase the risk of significant anxiety and depression. Parents who are stressed in every way may not have the bandwidth to take on the role of child therapist in addition to their other responsibilities.

I worry about our children's general wellbeing. Kids are less active than normal due to restricted sports and decreased commutes to school. Physical activity is an important component of overall health and known to improve mental health, sleep and learning. I worry that kids will snack a lot at home and gain weight, as it's been shown that most kids become overweight or obese during school vacations. If kids aren't vaccinated, attending regular checkups or dental cleanings, they may suffer other preventable complications.

We must keep studying and learning, but as a parent and a pediatrician, I think we should put risks in perspective. If 1/10,000 children experience a rare long-term complication, it matters. It's one child in a medium-sized town and doctors need a plan to optimize their care. But if 8% of children already have significant anxiety or depression before the pandemic and it increases 50% during the pandemic, it's 1 extra child out of an average class. This change will affect a generation of children on a different scale.

The other reason to focus on these more statistically likely complications is that we can mitigate these risks. We can organize our schedules to prioritize sleep and exercise to promote mental health. We can check in with our children and ask for help early if we think their mental health is struggling. We can prioritize preventive healthcare.

Let's do our best to follow facts, not fear.

Children with special healthcare needs

My first job after completing my training in pediatrics was working as a complex care pediatrician. Complex care pediatrics focuses on children who either have one condition (such as cerebral palsy or congenital heart disease) that requires care from multiple subspecialists or multiple conditions that make medical decision-making more challenging.

Parents who have children with special needs are facing more struggles than most during the pandemic. Many children have food allergies, and during a pandemic it may be even harder to find the few items they rely on. Many children have had long-planned surgeries canceled or delayed. Many children with breathing tubes, ventilators, or feeding tubes are facing supply shortages and lack of home nursing coverage.

Many children with developmental delay were making progress in speech, physical, and occupational therapy prior to the pandemic. Real, substantial progress was interrupted. Kids with cerebral palsy may be experiencing pain associated muscle spasms or outgrowing their braces without access to the therapists and clinics that help with these issues. Many children have significant behavioral problems or autism; these kids have had the structure of their days interrupted by school closures and their parents have less respite. I hope you know that many in our community are thinking of you and worried about you during this time.

While the struggles faced from the issues mentioned above seem insurmountable, thinking through the risks and benefits of various aspects of care can help prioritize the needs of your child to develop an action plan. As a pediatrician, I know you are so worried about your child getting sick from coronavirus. Some children are at higher risk for severe illness if they get sick. However, I would argue that the increased risk from coronavirus is probably similar to the increased risk we are used to tolerating and accommodating during every cold and flu season. Decision-making is very complex, and your primary care doctor or primary specialist can help by providing advice tailored to your specific situation. Currently, the most well-established risk factors include kidney disease, solid organ transplant recipients, cancer, obesity, serious heart conditions, sickle cell disease and type 2 diabetes. It's not clear yet if asthma or type 1 diabetes is a risk factor, but the CDC thinks children with medical complexity — including neurologic, genetic, metabolic or congenital heart disease — *might* be at higher risk.[22] I would strongly encourage you when you have choices to balance the risk of coronavirus with the risk of missing things.

We may overestimate the true risk of coronavirus due to what I would describe as a pandemic of fear. As I discussed previously, the true risk to children seems low, but children with complex health care needs are, of course, at higher risk. A handful of articles have examined this risk in greater detail by focusing on some of the most vulnerable children — those on chemotherapy and those with medical technologies.

Children on chemotherapy with active cancer are among some of the most vulnerable to viral illnesses, given their profound immunosuppression. While there aren't very many cases yet described in the literature (only 40), both studies found the course of illness to be mild for most children with cancer. Interestingly, these children seemed to be more likely to be symptomatic (with as many as 87% showing symptoms), but not more vulnerable to catching infection. Memorial Sloan Kettering tested all parents and found at least five families where the parents were asymptomatic and positive for active coronavirus infection, yet never transmitted the virus to their children despite close contact. Hospitalizations were mostly for monitoring of chemotherapy regimens, and children sick with coronavirus did well monitored at home. The one death observed was a child with sickle cell who was thought to have had a cardiac event.[23]

Another study looked at 48 children admitted to the pediatric ICU with coronavirus and 40 had underlying conditions. The most common underlying conditions were medically complex conditions requiring technology use (ventilators, tracheostomies and feeding tubes). Notably, in this series the authors state, "It is important to emphasize that the overall burden of COVID-19 infection in children remains relatively low compared with seasonal influenza."[24] I do not mean to minimize the risk. In my prior practice of extraordinarily vulnerable children with ventilators, prematurity, genetic syndromes and congenital heart disease, I saw again and again how hard regular respiratory viruses could be for some children. The children we should worry about the most are the ones who have required hospitalization in the past for viral illnesses. However, even for children with medical complexity, the risk of death seems small.

I don't have enough data to provide much specific information about other conditions like asthma and type 1 diabetes in children. The preliminary data indicates that asthma is not as much of a risk factor as we would have thought. Still, I'd like to recommend that, if your child has a chronic condition, you stay in close contact with your health provider. Adequate control of chronic conditions will decrease your risk should you get sick. Skipping visits with a doctor to decrease exposure may backfire if your condition is under poor control. Consider reaching out to your provider about telehealth or alternative visit options if you are concerned about exposures.

We have to balance the true but small risk of coronavirus with the true cost of extreme isolation for these children. Particularly if your local community transmission of coronavirus is low, activities like school, therapy sessions, and caregivers entering the home may be worthwhile. In a child who needs physical therapy, delaying it or stopping it may cause pain, developmental setbacks, and sometimes contractures that require surgery. In a child with autism or behavioral issues, missing opportunities to be in developmentally appropriate social situations and work with special education professionals or therapists may lead to extreme regressions. Given some of what we know about the critical period for language development, children who have hearing problems or speech problems that go unaddressed may miss important times for development. These are examples where the risks of missing things are very likely and potentially very significant.

So in a sense we are weighing IF your child gets sick and IF your child experiences a rare outcome against the cost your child will likely pay from remaining extensively isolated. Without knowing you and your family, I can't say what the risk is or what the correct answer is. This is what conversations with your doctors are for. If you don't feel confident talking with your doctors about these topics, consider reaching out to a complex care program for an appointment (remotely or in person). Some of the available programs are designed to take over primary care, but many of them, particularly in big academic centers, are accustomed to working as consultants and providing advice while encouraging your ongoing relationship with your primary care doctor. These are not easy decisions, but we wouldn't recommend and prioritize these services if they weren't truly important to your child. A child who misses medically important treatments will have a consequence. Children are resilient and some interventions can be delayed, but many things should not be.

The first few weeks and even the first few months of COVID-19, many imagined jumping back into their routine activities, but as we approach fall and winter without a vaccine, it's clear that's not how this is going to work. Indefinitely delaying some of these activities is a risk that may be underestimated by those less familiar with their conditions.

It's worth commenting on the pressure parents feel to choose the safest thing possible. When you hear of parents in your community making choices that are even more extreme than yours about physical distancing and limiting contacts, it's only natural to second-guess your choices. Less contact will undoubtedly decrease risk of illness, but you may bear other risks too.

You and your doctors should discuss any decisions you are struggling with so they can support you. And once you have made your decision, if others criticize or comment on it, you can respond by saying, "I've discussed this with my doctor and they agree I'm making a sensible choice for our family." Remember that, even if you are holed away protecting your family, you aren't alone and there are always resources available to you.

How to protect your newborn at home

Tiny babies are obviously vulnerable. Everyone knows this. They depend on us for everything and they even have a soft spot on their head where you can feel their brain directly through their skin. As a pediatrician, I have a lot of respect for the fragility of newborn babies. We see that they do not have much reserve of energy and strength for when they are sick. An ill baby can cope remarkably well and look fine until a sudden deterioration.

We have precautions in place to take any illness seriously in babies of this age. Fever should be treated like an emergency and a doctor involved if your child is sick. But what truly is the risk of coronavirus to babies?

We've seen that infants under one year, particularly those under two months, are at higher risk for hospitalization from coronavirus. However, we should keep in mind that doctors often admit young babies for observation if they are sick, and it's not clear what percentage of admissions have been precautionary. Data is limited in this age group but one study examined 19 healthy infants under 60 days admitted with coronavirus and found 6% required critical care, 5% required respiratory support, and the average length of stay was two days. So, while we certainly want to avoid exposing newborns to any virus, including coronavirus, infected infants have typically experienced mild symptoms.[25] Based on my review of the literature, I would suggest that the magnitude of the risk from coronavirus seems similar to other viruses that circulate in our community every year. It may even be that the risk to babies from coronavirus is slightly lower than influenza and RSV (while the risk of coronavirus for adults is much higher than these circulating viruses). For newborns, the risk of complications and hospitalizations from influenza and RSV is significant and matters. Many parents prior to the pandemic may have underestimated the impact of these viruses.

So, we must protect our infants from getting sick. I've personally dealt with this as a mother of two winter babies, and I'd like to share two anecdotes. First, when my dear friend had her second baby, she wanted to travel by plane to spend time with her parents during maternity leave. Prior to that, her baby hadn't been out much, as he was only six weeks. Likely en route he caught a virus, while at the grandparents 'house he developed fever and required hospitalization. He had blood draws and spinal taps that showed a common virus — enterovirus — had caused an infection that spread to his brain. He remained well, other than signs of a cold and fever, and was discharged after a couple of days. He's now 8 and a smart, charming and athletic boy, but I bring up this anecdote to remind you that we have always wanted to avoid newborns getting sick. What he went through was such a stress for my friend, and this story is relatively common. We also know that everyday viruses can cause more serious infections, though these are rare.

So you might think with this background I put my own children in a bubble, but no. When my son was born, 10 days before Thanksgiving, we had to decide whether to see family. I was worried that someone would get my little one sick. But my husband wanted to see his family and show off his new baby, and I was feeling ready to get out of the house. A few people were attending Thanksgiving who might not have been able to join the following year and it was important to my husband. So we decided to mitigate the risk as best we could.

For us, this meant asking everyone to have gotten the flu vaccine prior to Thanksgiving. While the baby was too young to be vaccinated, the flu vaccine decreased the likelihood of attendees exposing the baby to flu. We made sure that no one came sick or "sort of sick." And we asked people to wash their hands on arrival and before holding the baby. Also, when people were holding the baby, I would ask them to use a blanket over their clothing. This would protect their clothing from any baby spills and my baby from any fomites on their clothing.

I've heard from many parents — particularly new parents — that navigating these conversations with friends and families can be difficult. Your loved ones may disagree with the plan, but setting limits that you feel comfortable with is a normal part of parenting. I'll discuss this later on in more detail in the chapter *We don't make decisions in a bubble.*

Another strategy to protect our babies is to provide breastmilk. We know that breastmilk has antibodies to viruses circulating in the community and offers protection to small babies, and preliminary data shows this to be true for coronavirus as well. Often breastfeeding is difficult, but any quantity is likely protective. Lactating moms, like all moms during this time, may be more stressed with more demands and less support. Additionally, moms may have less access to resources like lactation consultants and pediatricians to help.[26] We should do our best to support them. We know that basics like sleep, a healthy diet with sufficient calories, and hydration are important components of successful breastfeeding.

Everyone loves celebrating new babies. Babies have an intoxicating smell and delightful cheeks. Many people want to hold them and kiss them. I would encourage you to be selective about who you allow to hold your baby. Just as we weigh the risk benefits on other big decisions during this time, every close contact is an exposure risk. As I mentioned above, I think the risk should your baby be infected with coronavirus is likely small but important. The benefit of others holding your baby will vary. Perhaps it's a close friend or family member who will be an important part of the baby's life and the benefit of exposure is substantial. Maybe it's a caregiver providing you with a break so that you can recover from giving birth or attend to some of your other responsibilities (like work or caring for siblings). I wouldn't hesitate to allow these contacts.

The contacts I would consider saying no to are the casual ones who want to hold the baby just for fun. Certainly the neighbor can come visit outside from 6 feet away wearing a mask and provide you an opportunity for some social engagement at virtually no risk to your baby, but how much do you benefit as a parent or baby from that person coming closer? Very little. In some ways, a pandemic is a great excuse to feel less guilt about saying no to contact that doesn't enrich the life of your family.

It's worth mentioning that cold sores pose a special risk to newborns. Herpes simplex virus (HSV) — the most common virus that causes recurrent cold sores — can be shed in the mouth of someone who carries the virus intermittently with no outward signs. Newborns are particularly vulnerable to HSV and it can cause life-threatening infection of the brain and spinal cord and seizures. Benign baby kisses from strangers have never been encouraged by pediatricians for this reason and shouldn't be permitted now either.

Once you have decided to allow contact, I would encourage you not to skip the basic step of washing hands. Another way to decrease baby's exposure risk is to use masks. Certainly babies learn a lot from looking at facial expressions, smiles, and seeing the production of words. But if someone is highly exposed and coming for a brief visit, I would require them to put a mask on.

When you take your baby out and about, I've found strangers are less likely to touch your baby if you use a carrier, since the tension of invading another adult's personal space seems a deterrent. If the baby is in a stroller, consider a loose cover — either a muslin blanket or a rain cover. Just be sure the baby is well ventilated and not too hot. Particularly with infants under 2 months, I would encourage you to be mindful of the risks of air travel or attending indoor events, though I'll talk more about the exposure of different activities later in the book.

A special challenge is when you have multiple kids. Parents of infants are always tired and often have difficulty balancing the needs of multiple children with the new baby's nap and feeding schedule. We must consider the siblings 'perspective and the parents 'perspective here. Maybe it's not a stretch to keep the kids home, or maybe it adds a lot of stress. Maybe the sibling is struggling with not getting out all of their energy and wreaking havoc at home. I can easily imagine situations where it makes sense to choose to keep older siblings home and situations where I'd send my older children to school.

We can decrease the risk of siblings infecting each other by focusing on basics. When kids come home, supervise a thorough hand washing. Ensure that siblings don't share water bottles and that the baby's toys, which are often in the baby's mouth, are either washed frequently or not played with by the sibling. Help the older sibling find ways to be involved with the baby without getting in the baby's face. For example, only touch or kiss the baby's feet or be mommy's special helper and get a diaper.

If baby gets sick despite your best efforts, try not to panic, but contact your doctor for advice.

Toddlers & Kids

As I discussed before, coronavirus is less dangerous for children than adults. However, the fallout from this pandemic is hitting children in so many other ways. It's worth diving into some of these secondary impacts so that we can protect our children.

During the pandemic, I've eaten enormously more snacks than before. I have been home and sitting in the kitchen while my son did his remote schooling, and when the snacks are right there it can be hard to resist. As a pediatrician, I worry about kids being less active than normal, snacking more, and gaining weight. Obesity in children is bad for their health — obviously for big things like diabetes and heart disease, but also for under-recognized problems that come with being heavy, such as decreased self-esteem, chronic joint pain and worse sleep. We also know that children who are overweight tend to stay overweight as adults.

Before the pandemic, the commute to school, sports and playtime at school were the biggest drivers of physical activity in children and all have plummeted. Besides simply driving weight up, being less active is associated with worse academic outcomes, worse sleep, worse behavior, and higher risk for mental health issues.

I worry about the children who have missed health maintenance visits. Just like we have seen decreases in new cancer diagnosis in adults during this time, I worry that we've missed important conditions in children. Decreased vaccination rates have received a lot of publicity and will leave children at risk for infections that could have been avoided.

Missed academic time is also a concern. Hopefully children will have opportunities to catch up on learning and efforts at remote schooling will improve. The disparities in access to high-quality education are more prominent than ever.

Pediatricians have always been skeptical of screentime. We know that children don't learn language as well from screens. In the past we've compared screentime to learning-rich alternatives such as school, playground or athletic time, and time with friends. Now as we think about screentime, we have to take a more nuanced approach. Innovations in content development have provided some great learning tools that can help prevent academic delays while at home.

Screens can be portals to connect with friends and family and provide essential social supports. Now they are also windows into school for many children. But screens can also provide opportunities for bullying or child predators. YouTube content can provide great enrichment (see resource list at the end of the book), but inappropriate content is only a few clicks away. Screentime must be supervised to be safe.

Mental health is important even in this age group. Kids can get depressed and anxious and the isolation, decreased physical activity, changes in routine, and stress during the pandemic hit all of us. In prior pandemics, children have had symptoms of post-traumatic stress disorder after lockdown, though not much is known about the intensity or duration of these symptoms. And certainly no pandemic since we've had this type of research has gone on so long.

Finally, social and emotional skill development is a concern of many parents. Can a child learn to smile and to talk if surrounded by people wearing masks? While we don't have a lot of data to guide our answers, I think these concerns may be overblown. It's easy to discredit the rich social environment of your home and family. Routine activities at home will help keep children learning social and emotional skills.

Later in the book we'll discuss how to mitigate the impact of each of these secondary effects of the virus on your family.

Tweens & Teens

Teenagers are at special risk from coronavirus. They act a bit more like adults in terms of their transmission and likelihood of getting sick. Teenagers seem slightly more likely to get, transmit and become sick than children under 10. A recent study of 65 children hospitalized for coronavirus in Queens, N.Y., showed that nearly half were teens — notable, given that small children typically have a harder time with viruses.[27] However, similar to young children, teenagers hospitalized with severe illness from coronavirus are likely to have multiple risk factors or multiple viruses. Teenagers can get MIS-C but the risk remains quite small. Teenagers remain at lower risk from the direct impacts of coronavirus than their parents.

I worry more about the secondary impacts of coronavirus on teenagers. Teenagers are at risk from decreased health screenings, obesity, academic delays and overdosing on screentime, just as I mentioned with younger kids. But because of the hormones and the critical developmental transition toward independence, teenagers are high risk for mental health and emotional problems during the best of times. Prior to the pandemic, the CDC estimated that teenagers compared to younger children have nearly double the risk of anxiety (6%) and three times the risk of depression (~10%)[28]. Because of this well-established risk, physicians routinely screen every child over 10 for depression, anxiety, suicidality, substance abuse and a number of other risk factors. Ideally these screenings are performed at every encounter, not just well child visits, because they are so important. Often clinicians can have a perspective and give adolescents the space to admit things they may not share with their parents.

But now, during this pandemic, teens are physically removed from their friends who are developmentally so essential to their world. And teens have interruptions in activities that are really important to them, whether it's sports, choir, prom or high school graduation. They have been preparing to leave the nest and now they are trapped. It seems like a setup for increased risk for all of these mental health problems — depression, anxiety, suicidality, substance abuse, and eating disorders.

But, and here's a big but, with risk and stress comes opportunity. Many parents of teens have unprecedented access to their children and opportunities to enrich their relationships. We know that these relationships can protect our children from suffering from stress, and we have an opportunity teach our teens coping mechanisms that will take them through the rest of their lives.

Another challenge in parenting teens during this time is you can't control them the same way you can a small child. You can't always keep them inside and monitor their activities. In asking them to socially distance, you have to use more sophisticated strategies. You need to motivate and convince them that social distancing is the right thing to do, rather than just trying to make them.

Some people say teens aren't that different from toddlers and in some ways it's true: If you make it into a power struggle, you'll likely make it worse. We'll talk more specifically about strategies to approach social distancing with your teen and help children with their mental health later in the book.

Coronavirus & Parents

What's the risk of coronavirus for most adults?

The pandemic has been going on for long enough that it's easy to lose perspective. What exactly is the risk to you if you catch coronavirus?

A case fatality rate (CFR) is easy to calculate — you simply divide the known deaths by the known cases. However, this number is flawed. Because we do not fully sample populations, we underestimate the number of cases, making the CFR higher than your risk of death should you become infected. Also, the CFR doesn't account for the future deaths that may occur in currently sick individuals.

The infection fatality rate (IFR) is what we'd like to know — how many deaths occur per all those infected with coronavirus. To have a more accurate sense of this requires surveillance of community transmission — mostly done by sampling for the presence of antibodies. Antibodies aren't a perfect proxy, as I discussed earlier — you may not have developed them yet or you may have lost them, particularly if you had a mild illness — but it gives us a sense of how many infections occurred in an area. Recently, a meta-analysis examined 24 different studies to try to

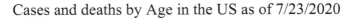

Cases and deaths by Age in the US as of 7/23/2020

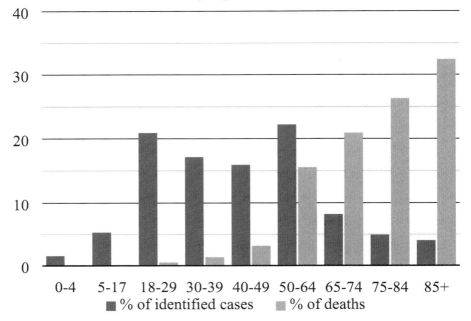

0-4   5-17   18-29 30-39 40-49 50-64 65-74 75-84   85+
■ % of identified cases   ■ % of deaths

provide the most accurate estimate and found the IFR to be 0.68% (with a range of 0.53-0.82%).[29]

It's easy to directly extrapolate this number and consider your child's school. Maybe there are 100 families, mostly with two parents each, and you think that if they all had coronavirus, one would die. This is a rather startling way to think of it and it's also incorrect.

We can't think about the overall CFR or IFR when we think of our individual risk because it varies considerably by age and comorbidity. The CDC reports that 80% or more of the deaths in the U.S. from coronavirus have been in individuals over age 65. Most of the cases are in younger individuals and most of the deaths are in older individuals, as shown in this chart based off numbers available on the CDC[30]

Because of the difficulties knowing with certainty how many individuals of each age group have been infected, I haven't seen helpful estimates of IFR by age in the United States. A study out of Sweden estimated the infection fatality rate at 0.0092% for adults 20-49 years old, 0.14% for adults 50-64, and 5.6% for individuals 65 and higher.[31] These rates mean that many parents with young children at home are at relatively low risk, though some would say Sweden is a healthier country than the U.S.

Notably, the risk of hospitalizations, some of which are lengthy and require prolonged recovery, is higher than the risk of death. However, the hospitalization chart varies by age in a similar fashion. Hopefully this is a reassuring reminder that the risk to your health should you get sick may be lower than you think. Still, as you can see, people of all ages have died in the U.S. of COVID-19 and it's worth avoiding.

If you have chronic medical conditions, your risk may be higher. Cancer, kidney disease, COPD, organ transplant, obesity, serious heart conditions and type 2 diabetes are currently listed as risk factors for severe coronavirus disease, but we are still learning more about individual conditions. Some other conditions, including ones that affect the lungs, heart, nervous or immune system, may predispose to more severe illness. It's best to check one of the risk evaluation tools available online and consult your doctor to best understand your specific risk.[32]

Pandemic-related stress

In the introduction, I asked you to take a minute to really check in with what is hardest for you about the pandemic because I have heard so many differing accounts.

For some families, the pandemic has not been that hard. Some parents have sufficient support and children have adapted well to remote learning. Perhaps there are no health problems that have caused extra stress. I have a feeling these lucky few are not reading this book, but if they are, I congratulate them.

For the rest of us, the pandemic has unleashed a Pandora's box of stress. In this section, first I'll talk about how the fear, lack of control, grief, decision fatigue and guilt can make this time harder for parents. Then, we'll dive into what we know about the risks of coronavirus for pregnant women, essential workers, parents of children with special health care needs, and grandparents.

FEAR & ANXIETY

Hopefully by now you believe me that the direct risk of coronavirus and MIS-C is relatively low for children. Still, fear of coronavirus is normal. Fear is an evolutionary drive to help us avoid danger. Coronavirus is dangerous. So it's normal for fear to activate cortisol and other stress hormones involved in the fight-

or-flight cascade. Our hearts run faster and our palms sweat. When these pathways rise to higher levels, we can have trouble sleeping, feel palpitations or shortness of breath, or even experience panic attacks.

This fear is not helpful in our day-to-day interactions living during a pandemic. We need to be thoughtful and level-headed. So how can we rein in fears that can overwhelm us?

Stopping habits that worsen anxiety is a good first step. Excess caffeine and poor sleep are well known to increase anxiety. Social media platforms like Facebook and Instagram can also be detrimental (though I continue to post there regularly!). Alcohol, smoking and skipping meals can also trigger anxiety.

Adding protective habits like exercise can be another way to feel better. When I am at my busiest and most worried, it's easy to feel that I don't have time to exercise, but what I've learned is I don't have time not to exercise, because getting moving makes me more effective at tackling my life and improves my mood dramatically. Exercise is an evidence-based way to cope with stress.

Mindfulness and meditation can decrease fear. Busy people often don't give themselves time to really experience the emotions we are faced with. If you give yourself even two or three minutes to sit with these uncomfortable feelings, sometimes they can feel much more manageable. If you're feeling scared, writing down everything you are worried about can be cathartic. Journaling can allow you to put your thoughts down on paper and feel relief from the never-ending flow of thoughts, which can be overwhelming.

For many people, fear can be really overwhelming. We can know the facts but still see risk in all our interactions. If you consistently feel overwhelmed by intrusive thoughts and fears during this time, please know you are not alone in this and you may be experiencing situational anxiety. If this is impeding your ability to function — to care for your children, go to the grocery store, sleep, or maintain core relationships — please consider seeking help.

LACK OF CONTROL

For many of my friends, one of the hardest parts about the pandemic is our inability to plan ahead. We don't know what school will look like or when we'll be able to go on a vacation. We don't know how our kids will cope or whether our job will still exist.

Looking to your support network to discuss this stress is an important outlet. By talking through things and understanding that you aren't alone in these feelings, the situation can seem more manageable and promote a sense of understanding and control.

Again, journaling can be a help. Once you have a long list of all the things frustrating you, you can add another column to consider the different options of what can happen. What you'll see is that, although you can't possibly have a robust plan for every scenario, you can imagine ways things can come together.

Here's are a few of my examples:

No vacation plans

— last-minute trips, do without, drive somewhere, staycation.

Unclear school plans

— remote school, in-person school, mix of both.

Job plans

— go back to work as normal, no job for a while, find remote work.

No activities for kids in the winter

— running wind sprints in the basement, YouTube Yoga, Zoom karate class.

Another thing that helps if you're feeling out of control is to find a task to immerse yourself in. That can promote a state of consciousness referred to as flow and popularized by psychologist Mihaly Csikszentmihalyi in his best-selling book. For me, I often find flow cleaning or organizing a part of my home. Exercise, art, sports, puzzles, cooking or playing with your kids are all examples of ways you can find outlets to feel in control.

Consuming a lot of media about coronavirus may help you feel better in the moment — you are up to date and in the loop. But in the long run, this constant flow of somewhat sensationalized information may worsen your feelings of powerlessness.

GRIEF

Another theme in how and why parents struggle during this time is grief. We had worked to set our lives up in a certain way. My daughter's daycare was providing a rich developmental environment and allowed me to have the work-life balance I intentionally selected. My son had made it halfway through kindergarten and had begun really enjoying it and establishing new friendships.

Then daycare closed and my work-life balance was wrecked. I wanted to continue working but couldn't sacrifice the quality of my daughter's care. My son's school went remote and his friends scattered. Although his schools went above and beyond, remote instruction for a kindergartner is incomplete, and we still were disappointed to miss his first class play, his teddy bear picnic and other kindergarten milestones.

I use these relatively trivial examples on purpose because it's easy during this stressful time to feel grief about things you were looking forward to that you are missing. I know many children were heartbroken over graduations and canceled sporting events and many adults are distraught over missed vacations. It's also tempting to immediately dismiss this kind of grief because people are struggling in much more serious ways. The death toll, the unemployment, the frontline workers coping with such stress, the individuals dealing with non-COVID-related health crises during this time all matter more than my son's teddy bear picnic.

However, allowing yourself to experience grief can help you to process it and release it. Even if your problems are anthills next to others 'mountains, they are your problems and exist in their own right. Identifying your grief can help you process it and work through the stages.

- **Denial**

  - It can feel like a healthy coping mechanism to ignore grief and hope it will go away. But often you still carry the stress and it will find ways to affect you. I got stuck here in the height of the pandemic in NYC — I couldn't process all the grief so I focused on day-to-day activities.

- **Anger**

- It's natural to feel mad when you don't get your way, even if it's illogical. We all have a tiny toddler in our brains. Sometimes we struggle to find outlets for feelings of anger in our lives as parents — I have seen great coverage of Mom-Rage in The New York Times[33].

- **Bargaining**
  - If only coronavirus hadn't hit NYC when it did. If only we had locked down earlier. If only we had gone straight to recommending universal masking right away. If only the vaccine developed for MERS had been completed, we'd be closer to a vaccine. While these thoughts are often based in fact, they aren't helpful.

- **Depression**
  - A common stage includes deep feelings of loss or being overwhelmed by your grief. Sadness and tearfulness are part of this stage, as are feelings of numbness and disconnection.

- **Acceptance**
  - Finding peace with where you are.

- **Finding meaning**
  - Using your experience to help others or start a new path for yourself.

We all have so many reasons to grieve during this time. It takes energy, time, and emotional reserves to grieve. When we don't have those things, grief can be even more difficult to process and the stages can be more difficult to move through.

This why you'll see that, later in the book, I encourage you to prioritize your self-care as parents. Not only does it allow you to be a role model for your child, it allows you to be a healthier person and a better parent.

DECISION FATIGUE

The last category of coping difficulties I'd like to address is decision fatigue. Suddenly every decision we make is laced with uncertainty *and* the significance life or death. Every day we make dozens of decisions as straightforward as whether to go to the grocery store, see a loved one, or allow your child a playdate. Now each of these everyday decisions is a moral dilemma.

This is exhausting. The stress of each decision adds up — particularly because there is no clear or easy answer. If you choose to *do* activities that increase your family's exposure, you face the increased risk of coronavirus. If you *don't* do things you want to do, you're not living the life you'd prefer.

Physicians deal with making decisions in the face of uncertainty all the time. In fact, there's a whole literature showing that we are human too. We make better decisions earlier in the day, prescribing fewer unnecessary antibiotics and more cancer screening before we're tired.[34] Distractions, interruptions, and running on "autopilot" also impact the quality of our decisions. Yet we do our best and have some strategies to try to do better.

Here are some ideas I recommend for coping with decision fatigue:

- **Give yourself a break.**

    - You may need more time to process and make decisions. Sometimes, sleeping on a tough decision really can help.

- **Limit your decisions.**

    - Successful people are often people of habits — having the same breakfast everyday, the same dinners in rotation, or wearing your favorite outfit over and over can save mental energy. Think Steve Jobs with his black turtleneck and jeans.

- **Limit your options.**

    - Rather than considering every carseat on the market, it can be helpful to choose among the top few you see recommended. This is similar to the Pareto principle. You can often get 80% of the results by investing 20% of the effort. Some decisions are important and require

100% thought, but many everyday decisions will be good enough when done quickly.

- **Develop an algorithm.**
  - Doctors often follow evidence-based protocols to help them decide about testing or treatment. Then, instead of deciding from scratch every time, we decide, is this a situation that fits with the protocol or not. This saves us the time of rethinking the entire protocol each time.

- **Have a decision-making strategy.**
  - I'll describe this in more detail later in the book.

- **Trust your gut, your doctor, or your loved ones.**
  - Delegate or ask for help making decisions.

- **Try not to second-guess your decisions.**
  - When making a challenging decision, I often tell myself the reason it's so tough is that both options are good. This helps put the decision into perspective. We tend to worry most about the decisions where both options are nearly equivalent.

I'll try to give you more strategies to approach coronavirus decisions later in the book, but recognizing the toll all of these decisions take may help you understand why you are struggling. Along these same lines, seeing our communities in crisis can be very stressful. Even if our families are safe, seeing high numbers rolling in from our communities can be very difficult, particularly for sensitive or empathetic individuals.

GUILT

A lot of parents suffer carrying unhealthy feelings of guilt. Some guilt – natural guilt – is a consequence of something we did or failed to do. When you forget someone's birthday or snap at your children, you may feel guilt. This guilt tends to be transient.

Toxic guilt is a sense of feeling like a failure or as if you've let other people down. I worry that some parents feel guilty because of their untenable situation. We can't possibly meet all the demands on our time if we are working from home, with less childcare, and more schooling responsibilities than normal. Some parents may feel guilty that their children are missing out on the life planned pre-pandemic. But acknowledging that you feel guilty about something that isn't your fault can be the first step in feeling better.

Sometimes just feeling that illogical feeling can help dissipate the tension. While it may sound cheesy, I think it's helpful to visualize letting go of this guilt. Imagine blowing out a bubble full of guilt and watching it float away. Or think of a duck in a rainstorm. The guilt is like the water that beads up and runs off the duck's back.

Another technique that may help is to think of some mantras.

"I'm doing the best I can"

"I can do hard things"

"Perfect is the enemy of good"

"At least we're healthy"

I find that having a quick catch-phrase is helpful because unwanted negative feelings can flare up often when you are feeling really stretched. If you can't shake feelings of failure and worthlessness, it could be a sign of depression.

Existential guilt is a negative feeling that arises out of perceived injustice in the world. Survivor guilt is an example. Though we know it's not our *fault,* we question why we would survive when someone else didn't. I worry about healthcare providers feeling this as it can be associated with trauma and a symptom of post-traumatic stress disorder.

Some people have had a nice experience of the pandemic and may be happier than ever. Maybe working from home provides them with more time with their family or their children are thriving with more time. Sometimes comparing their positive experience with how much suffering is happening elsewhere, they may feel guilty. While it's easy to poke fun at such an admirable position, again the first step is identifying the feeling. If you feel guilty about winning the pandemic, how about challenging yourself to give back. Small actions such as supporting friends or checking on elderly neighbors may help you feel better. Many charities need more help than ever.

WHEN TO ASK FOR HELP

The easy answer regarding when to seek help with your mental health is early and often. While anxiety, depression and grief are normal reactions to a pandemic, if you want help coping, help is available. It's easy to think of mental health problems as black and white — you have them or you don't — but the reality is that there is a lot of gray.

Some people may have been thriving despite minor depression or anxiety because of good supports and coping mechanisms prior to the pandemic. Now the added stress and anxiety coupled with the decreased supports have undoubtedly pushed some into a place where they want or need professional help.

Parents who are feeling depressed or anxious often feel quite overwhelmed and as if they don't have the time to get help. Mostly, though, time invested in feeling better will pay off. Feeling better can provide you more time and energy to tackle the challenges in your path.

Another common excuse I hear is, I can't prioritize seeing a mental health professional when my children need me. But I see right through this. If a parent is suffering, the child will suffer too. You have an opportunity to be a role model to your child and escape the trap of being a parent who is a martyr.[35]

If your feelings are making it so you can't function or you are suffering, please don't hesitate. For all the energy you are spending protecting your physical health — even reading a book about coronavirus — investing in your mental health is just as important *and* connected to your physical health too.

On the back of most insurance cards is a phone line for reaching someone to help you find a mental health professional covered by your insurance. If that doesn't work, your primary care doctor can likely recommend someone or even get you started on a plan to feel better in the meantime. Other resources exist, depending on where you live. Please see my list of resources in the back of the book.

What are the risks to pregnant women?

Pregnancy is often a state of heightened emotions. Even a healthy pregnancy during a normal time can feel like a rollercoaster of excitement, fear, hope, joy and sadness. So experiencing pregnancy during a pandemic is a special treat. A pandemic infects every part of your pregnancy experience and it's unfair. Additionally, you may be more likely than non-pregnant women to have your normal reactions to the situation (i.e., fears and sadness) become overwhelming (i.e., clinically significant anxiety and depression) and all of the advice from the prior sections about your mental health and wellbeing apply.

Given how common mental health issues are in pregnancy, most OB-GYNs are well prepared to counsel you should you need help. I've had friends and parents of my patients hesitate to seek mental healthcare while pregnant because of the possibility of risk with medication. While this is a complex issue, this fear should not be a barrier. You should explore your options because many are safe in pregnancy and while breastfeeding.

Now I'd like to review what we know so far about the coronavirus in pregnancy. As someone who has done a lot of medical research, I am well aware of the historic gaps in research. Children, women, pregnant women, and minorities are all under-researched. And the pandemic has brought this to our attention. At a time when we know a lot about coronavirus and more than 4,000 research papers have been submitted, only a handful of small studies have been published about pregnant women.

This is somewhat reassuring. If ICUs were full of pregnant women, I think healthcare providers would have prioritized the research. But as it stands, pregnant women stand in a gray zone of risk. Certainly pregnancy is a time when your lung capacity is reduced due to your large belly and your blood has a propensity to clot due to your hormone balance. Additionally, pregnancy is a known immunocompromised state and viruses like chickenpox, which are well tolerated normally, can cause serious illness in pregnant women. Each of these factors lead us to have legitimate concern about the wellbeing of pregnant women should they become infected with coronavirus.

The literature does suggest pregnant women are at increased risk for severe illness if they get coronavirus. However, the risk doesn't seem to be entirely out of proportion to other viruses that women get, such as the flu. The MMWR report from the CDC from June 2020[36] reported pregnant women had nearly double the risk of requiring intensive care as age-matched non-pregnant women (1.5% vs. 0.9%) and slightly higher risk of needing a ventilator (0.5% vs. 0.3%). We don't really have the data to look at hospitalization rates yet since the available data doesn't state whether hospitalization was due to healthy labor.

It's also worth considering that, during the first four months of the pandemic reported in this report, testing for coronavirus varied considerably. Most places could test only the sickest patients at the beginning. Some places, such as NYC, began screening every woman admitted for labor with coronavirus and during their surge found 87% of positive cases identified had no symptoms[37]. Other places had only enough testing access to test symptomatic cases. Certainly we can imagine these two testing scenarios would lead to different results. Looking at every pregnant woman who tests positive with universal testing, it's likely that women do better than the averages reported above. But if we test only women who present as symptomatic, they are already a higher risk group for complications.

To put the risk in context, it's helpful to compare COVID-19 to influenza. During the H1N1 influenza pandemic, pregnant women were at extremely increased risk — despite making up 1% of the population, they made up 5% of the deaths[38]. The risk of ICU admission for flu was 7x that of age-matched non-pregnant women (remember, so far it seems 50% higher in COVID-19). While coronavirus is not the flu and comparisons are fraught with difficulty, it's worth noting that the flu vaccination and prompt treatment with antiviral therapies have been recommended for pregnant women. Despite these recommendations, only 54% of pregnant women in 2016-2017 were vaccinated for the flu[39].

While we can dig further into the available data, I am not sure it's productive to do so. In my opinion, a typical pregnant woman should assume you are at slightly increased risk for severe outcomes should you get sick. We don't know how likely other possible coronavirus outcomes are, such as preterm labor or preeclampsia. The risk is not so high that I think you need to panic. If you do become sick with coronavirus, extra ultrasounds to check on the baby may be indicated and many of the same treatments can be used as in non-pregnant patients. Ideally we can take measures to protect you from infection.

Every pregnant woman should have a healthcare provider she trusts. And since every woman is in a unique position with her family, workplace, health conditions, and local incidence of coronavirus, her provider is the best suited to give specific advice about what to do. What's clear for everyone is that concerns about coronavirus are not a good reason to avoid attending routine prenatal visits or delivering at a hospital. Doctors, nurses and other health providers should be doing everything to protect you from transmission, including wearing masks and using protective apparel.

Policies regarding support persons vary considerably, even within the same hospital system over the course of the pandemic, reflecting the risk of virus transmission in the local community. While it can be upsetting if the rules are inconvenient, if they limit you to one support person or require that the support person stay for the duration and not leave, please know that these rules are designed to protect the pregnant women, newborn babies, nurses, midwives, and doctors working in these units.

I do encourage that, whatever you do, you do your best to avoid getting coronavirus the two weeks before getting birth. Practices have varied across the country, but certainly however you give birth, you'll be at higher risk for complications if you are sick. Hospital policies may be an inconvenience if you have active coronavirus during delivery. You may be a risk to others you encounter at the hospital, most importantly your newborn baby.

Deciding what to do if you have coronavirus and a newborn is a personal decision. You have to see what your options are and consider the opinions of your co-parent, family, and doctors at the time. Certainly if a pregnant woman is sick with coronavirus, she may require a level of care that requires her to separate from her baby. Most pregnant women hopefully will not be so sick and some may even be asymptomatic. If this is your situation, I hope you will have a choice in what to do and be able to discuss it with your doctor, who can provide the up-to-the-minute accurate information. When the data doesn't provide a clear answer, shared decision-making is the best way to approach making an evidence-guided choice that's right for you.

I would just say that, given what we know now, if it were me and I were asymptomatic or mildly symptomatic with coronavirus, I would not choose to separate from my newborn. While the CDC and AAP encourage separation, many other health organizations internationally do not (WHO, obstetric leaders in Canada, UK, Australia, and New Zealand). I would wash my hands and mask, and take precautions to avoid giving it to the baby.

While choosing not to separate is a risk and your newborn may get sick and suffer complications, I think the risk is small and outweighed by the benefits of being together. I know that if I were to separate from my newborn, I would experience a lot of stress, sadness, and anxiety. The benefit of being together is substantial for skin-to-skin contact and to facilitate breastfeeding. Depending on your priorities, beliefs and values and your logistic options for who will care for your baby if separated from you, you may make a different decision. That's the entire point of shared decision-making.

Breastfeeding or providing pumped breastmilk after delivery is likely helpful, as it will provide some protection by transfer of antibodies. If you are sick at the time of the delivery, it is likely that at least some of your early antibodies may have transferred to the baby by your placenta prior to delivery. None of this protection is foolproof. But it may help.

Another pregnancy-related topic on many people's minds right now is whether pregnancy should be put off due to the risk of coronavirus. My answer to this question is a definitive no. If you want to grow your family and that's important to you, we know that waiting is not always a benign idea. As women get older, having a baby can be much harder or even impossible. In a sense, what you are choosing between is a theoretic risk — IF you get pregnant and IF you have a complication as compared to an actual risk that IF you delay pregnancy, risk of difficulty getting pregnant will certainly increase. That said, deciding to grow your family is an incredibly complex and personal decision and only you know what's right. Your doctors can also help you consider the individual risks and benefits here.

What's the risk to essential workers?

Parents who are working in positions where they are highly exposed to coronavirus — in a hospital or clinic, in a grocery store or school — face additional considerations during this time. Often these individuals worry the most about bringing the virus home to their family. I know so many physicians who have chosen to live apart from their families to protect them. This sort of decision is not to be taken lightly, nor is it feasible for many families.

It's worth noting that during the peak of coronavirus in NYC, healthcare workers were less likely to test positive for the virus than others in the community.[40] Many assume this is because of the knowledge of infection control procedures, adherence to physical distancing recommendations and access to appropriate protective apparel. I don't think this should keep you from taking precautions to protect your family, but I hope it can give you a peace of mind.

When friends ask me what they should do to mitigate the risk of bringing a virus home, I recommend strict adherence to appropriate safety precautions at work. Sometimes in workplaces, peer pressure can encourage you to slack in your adherence, particularly when it's annoying or inconvenient. Keeping up your daily motivation to wear your mask, wash your hands, and maintain distance from others while doing your job will not be easy but it will be necessary. You may be in a workplace where others are making different choices, but remaining focused on what you've decided for your family is important.

Practical considerations include the following:

- If possible at work, you should wear clothing that can be washed.

- Take off your shoes before entering your home.

- Sanitize high-touch surfaces like your phone, ID or keys.

- Assume your work bag is dirty and keep it somewhere away from other belongings.

- If you wear contacts, switching to glasses may provide more eye protection and decrease your likelihood of touching your eyes.

- If you have long hair, consider pulling it back. Washing or covering your hair will decrease your risk of carrying home germs on your hair.

It's worth noting that some essential workers are coping with high levels of stress. Just being out in the community at a high level of exposure can cause a lot of anxiety. Will I bring this home to my family? Working in a position of caring for coronavirus patients when a hospital is overwhelmed can cause traumatic levels of stress. Please know that you aren't alone in these feelings. Talking with others about how you are coping (or not coping) can help. If you are really struggling, seeking professional advice may be necessary. In the resources section, I'll highlight a few specific resources if you need more help.

Parents of children with special healthcare needs

I already have a section about your children, but I know from working with hundreds of families like yours over the years there are some things I should say.

Being a parent of a child with special healthcare needs can be isolating. Sometimes it's harder to bond when people aren't going through the same thing you are. Your child may not adapt well to last-minute social outings. When it comes to childcare or babysitters, the pool of candidates you can trust may be much smaller.

But I don't need to tell you this. Because you know this — it's your life. What I need to tell you is that I am worried about you. You are under more strain than the average parent, holding your family to higher standards of isolation, and you have less help.

So please take care of yourself. This applies to everyone, but especially to you. You may have to lower your expectations or say yes to offers of help that you normally say no to. While your child may need to be out and about more for appointments, therapies or potentially for school when other schools are closed, please remember that adult-to-adult transmission seems more common than child-to-adult, particularly for children under 10. So, while it's easy to think you're already exposed to the class or the adults working with your child through your child, I would continue to take precautions to prevent adult-to-adult transmission — most importantly, distance and masking. Precisely because you do so much for your child, we all need you to stay healthy.

It's always a good idea to have a care plan with contact information for all the doctors, a list of all the appointments, medications, and feeding instructions for your child, but it's even more important now. I know so many parents who don't have backup caregivers trained, but if you get sick, your child will still need help. Now is the time to make this plan.

If you haven't seen your child's doctor in a while, please schedule a telemedicine visit. Your child will benefit from having chronic issues under better control and a full stock of supplies and medications. Be sure to bring a list of questions for your doctor and ask if there are coronavirus-related things you should know about your child's care. For example, nebulizers may aerosolize virus more effectively and are discouraged for routine asthma care during the pandemic. There may be other issues you haven't thought of to consider and your doctor can help.

What about the grandparents?

Without a doubt, grandparents are the highest risk individuals in most families for coronavirus. Age alone is a risk factor for more severe disease, hospitalization, and death. Age is also a risk factor for many of the high-risk conditions such as high blood pressure, diabetes, heart disease and obesity.

With school and childcare centers closed, grandparents have been called on to fill the gaps and have been a fantastic resource for many families. However, as things open up more and more, we must remember that grandparents are more vulnerable to severe courses of coronavirus. This can leave families with difficult choices between opportunities for their children to get out of the house and the desire to stay in close contact with grandparents. These decisions are not easy.

Often I've seen adults parenting their grownup parents during this epidemic. This overwhelmingly comes from a good place. Adult children love their parents and don't want them to get sick. However, I think that, after ensuring an accurate understanding of the risks, we need to respect the choices that the grandparents make during this time. Sometimes we watch people make decisions we don't agree with.

This is easier said than done. Early in my career in pediatrics, I had to grow in my ability to embrace shared decision-making.

Working in complex care, many of my patients had serious brain injuries. These injuries caused difficulty coordinating the muscles of their mouth and throat, such that swallowing food sometimes went down "the wrong way" into the lungs rather than the stomach. When this aspiration happens, it can cause chronic wheezing or recurrent infections of the lungs. Over time it can lead to a decline in lung function or even death. However, sometimes their parents would choose to feed their children by mouth despite the known risk of aspiration.

My desire to tell these parents what to do was strong. You may even have strong opinions based on what you've read above. "Don't feed the child!" I wanted to say. "Use a feeding tube. It's safe and may help you avoid hospitalization." However, with good mentorship, an inquisitive nature, and an open mind, I learned about shared decision-making and the importance of active listening.

When I was able to listen to some of the reasons parents wanted to continue feeding, it really opened my eyes to understanding things. "When I feed my daughter, it's the only part of my day caring for her that feels normal" or "When my son eats, he seems more expressive and connected more than any other time of day." When I listened to these parents 'experiences, it helped me understand the context they were using to make decisions.

I also learned more about their values and the strengths in their relationships with their children. It allowed me to support these families and be a better doctor. In the end, it's not my life and, looking back, I am embarrassed that I could have thought I knew the right decision for a family after spending a few hours with them. Parents are making the best decisions they can for their family and my role as a doctor is to educate them and support them in their journey.

So with this context, it's no surprise that when my own father said "I've been looking forward to this trip for years and I may not have the chance at another one," I had practice at asking questions before offering opinions. Had he considered the risks and did he understand the facts? Yes. So, I can accept his choice and respect his decision. Who knows if he'll go, but at the end of the day it's his life.

Mitigating the impact
of the pandemic

Prepare and take stock

Some of the first posts I shared about coronavirus for family and friends included advice about preparing your home for the pandemic.

Even though we've been dealing with this for months at this point, it's still practical to be stocked with at least two or preferably four weeks of essential medicine, formula and diapers. Having a supply of nonperishable food your family will eat can also help reduce the urgency of visits to the grocery store. While we don't anticipate more lockdowns, if you or a family member gets sick, you may be stuck at home.

What would happen if someone in your house got sick tomorrow? Practically, they'd need to isolate away from the other family members. They'd need their medicine, food, drinks, and ideally their own bathroom. If it's a child, they will need one caregiver, and the other children may need a separate caregiver. Is this your plan? This plan is ideal for protecting everyone in your family and allowing some to return to school and work sooner, but it's not feasible for many families, including my own. Since my family happens to be low-risk for severe outcomes from coronavirus and able to work remotely, we would choose not to isolate from each other.

But I would ask you to consider what happens if both adults get coronavirus. This has happened across the country and it's not a good situation. When two COVID-19-positive adults are admitted to the hospital, their children are left without care. In many situations, emergency foster care will not accept a potentially coronavirus-positive child, so these children are admitted to the hospital for emergency childcare until a parent recovers. Can you imagine how a child would feel? Let's try to find a friend or family member who might be willing to help before the situation comes up. It's a big ask, but it's important.

Now to take stock of your family. In the prior sections, we spoke about who in your family might be the most vulnerable based on age and underlying conditions. Sometimes underlying conditions can be improved. Are there are ways to improve your health in case you get sick?

Unfortunately, there is no evidence supporting the use of "immune boosting" supplements. While elderberry has been shown to have antiviral activity against influenza, we don't know if it's effective against coronavirus. Elderberry is also known to increase pro-inflammatory cytokines - immune system activators. However, with coronavirus, some of the most severe cases have been due to "cytokine storm" or overly vigorous reactions. In children, no studies have been published about the long-term safety of elderberry. There is no evidence of benefit and a possibility of harm. I recommend you pass.

Early in the pandemic, zinc lozenges were promoted as a way to block the receptors and decrease your likelihood of catching coronavirus. While this is possible, it's unlikely to make a big difference. Zinc is well-known to change the way you taste and smell, so don't be surprised if you use a lozenge and think you may have a symptom of coronavirus.

Of all the supplements you could consider to boost your immune system, vitamin D makes the most sense. Statistically, vitamin D deficiency is quite common, and we know that vitamin D plays a role in healthy immunity. Studies have tried to connect low vitamin D with worse outcomes from coronavirus, but it's not clear. Even if there were a correlation, we do not have evidence that low vitamin D causes worse outcomes from coronavirus or that taking vitamin D supplements would help prevent severe coronavirus infections.

The most evidence-based way to be healthier is to routinely prioritize your wellness. A healthy varied diet is the best way to get your nutrients. Sleep of adequate quantity and quality and maintaining a healthy weight and activity level will support your immune system.

With stress and excess time at home, many have gained weight, but obesity may increase your risk some. If you are motivated and feeling ready, you can take steps towards eating more healthfully or exercising more. This is especially important if you have high blood pressure. Increasing physical activities or losing a small amount of excess weight can have substantial impact on your heart health.

A healthy lifestyle will also promote your mental health. It's a good idea to consider the mental health of all your family members. Start with yourself and be honest.

Check- in: How are you doing?

As parents, we set the example for our children. When we become unbalanced, our homes will suffer too. During the pandemic, the crushing stress has led so many people to function worse than normal at a time when we need to be on our game. When you are burned out, climbing out of that hole feels impossible. But I would say that, more than any other advice I give in this book, prioritizing parental self-care is essential.

Self-care has become a bit polarizing as a term because of how broad it is. For some, it conjures images of a yoga retreat and others an extra moment in the bathroom or pantry. As a physician, the common-sense actions I recommend are wellness basics. These include getting sunlight and activity every day, eating regular meals, taking a shower, and sleeping regular hours. If you can maintain the basic framework of your day, you are well on your way to promoting your mental health.

We don't have the same level of childcare and alone time we did before the pandemic. This pinch directly hits parents and our personal time. I used to work while my children were in school and daycare, and now mostly I work after they go to bed – which is when I used to relax. My physical activity only fits if I get to it first thing in the morning or if I do it with my children. I'm not pretending it's easy to prioritize these basics, but it's important.

Once you've gotten the basics in place, the next layer of self-care includes connection with others. For some more extroverted people, this may feel like part of your basic needs, but for some of us who hide away typing behind a screen, we need reminding. Data suggest that loneliness is a huge component of parental stress.

There are loads of other ideas for how to promote your wellness as a parent — yoga, journaling, gratitude, meditation, and disconnecting. These are great ideas, but at a time when so many parents feel so strapped, I have trouble suggesting them. If you can incorporate some of these, great. But if not, another strategy is to try to decrease your load.

There are only 24 hours in a day and many of the demands on parents are fixed (work, childcare, meal prep, laundry/housework). Some strategies can increase your efficiency. Batching, collecting similar tasks such as cooking, paying the bills, or laundry and doing them in a burst, can save time by preventing you from losing time and energy switching gears. But if you feel you can't get everything done, there are really three main options to help.

- **Recruit more help from your household**

    - Obtaining more help from your children can be enriching and educational. My son now knows more about laundry and can handle more of his routine than before the pandemic. Undoubtedly this is good for him. We know giving children autonomy when they are ready for it increases their self-esteem and likelihood of taking on more challenges. Often there is another co-parent you can work with to find a better balance.

- **Decrease your expectations**

    - We hold ourselves to exceptionally high standards. The quality of meals, amount of child enrichment, and tolerance of mess are a few examples of things that could stand to give a little. Sometimes when these things give, parents can preserve more time for themselves. And when parents are have a break, sometimes they find their efficiency improves.

- **Obtain more help from outside your household**
    - We'll touch more on babysitters, daycare, childcare, and school in the sections to come, but every family should consider whether the parents need more help.

Now that we know where we stand, let's move on to the hard stuff.

Making the best decisions for YOUR family

When my husband and I made the decision to purchase a house outside of New York City, the prior owners left behind a trampoline. The trampoline is big, above ground and in fair condition at best. We had a decision to make — should we have it removed or let the kids play?

As a pediatrician, I know the risks of trampolines. If you ask me, "Should I get a trampoline?" the answer is a resounding no! The professional societies of both pediatricians and orthopedists have strong statements against their use. 300,000 children had injuries requiring a medical visit due to a trampoline in 2018. Some of these injuries are minor, but 53 fractures occur per 100,000 children over a year. A handful of these injuries (0.5%) are devastating, life-changing injuries to the spine.

So, I got rid of it, right? Well, here's the time to be honest — I did not. As much as I reviewed the statistics available about the risks, I also considered the benefits. I have young rule-abiding children who are always supervised and tend to avoid risks. Since 75% of trampoline injuries occur when multiple people bounce at the same time, I knew I could significantly decrease my children's risk by having rules. Injuries on home trampolines also tend to be less severe than those at jump parks. For my kids, I felt the risks were manageable.

I thought about the benefits. For my children, particularly during the pandemic lockdown, the benefits were substantial. Without their friends, my kids were more sedentary. I could play tag with them or race with them for a while when I had the energy, but they would lose interest. They are too young to really engage in sports, biking or jogging, and hardly get their heart rate up from video sports classes. The trampoline is a way to get them moving. This exercise helps them sleep, improves tantrums and behavioral problems, increases appetite and helps with their core strength. The deciding factor: They love it.

We kept the trampoline. I bring up this story because it's an example of how we approach decisions in real life. We think about the risks and benefits specific to our family and we consider ways to mitigate or decrease the risks. Emily Oster, the bestselling author of *Cribsheet* and *Expecting Better,* described this framework in her Parent Data newsletter to encourage parents to thoughtfully approach decisions. Pose the question first as specific as possible. Evaluate the risks and benefits. Consider how you can mitigate the risks. Then decide.

For our children specifically, we felt the risk was in a range we could accept, and we could further mitigate this risk to promote safety. We bounce one at a time, under supervision, no flips or "moves," we don't go on the trampoline if it's raining, and if anyone isn't listening or is acting out on the trampoline, it is closed for the day. The benefits for us were worth it. This works for us … but I still won't recommend you get one.

Decision-making sounds so easy in this framework, but unfortunately, it's not. There is high social pressure to do the safest thing possible to protect your child from harm, at all times. Even sharing my controversial trampoline decision, I wonder if you will judge me or think less of me as a parent and a pediatrician. But truly I believe that the best person to make these sorts of decisions is the parent.

Individuals who challenge your decisions as being too conservative or too liberal often do so out of a place of fear.

Sometimes these fears aren't about you. Your decision as a parent can make others second guess their own choices.

Or your decision may cause others who care about your well-being to be concerned. In fact, that's why I don't want you to get a trampoline. Your child could get hurt — a broken arm or worse. I worry that you'll underestimate the risk and make a decision you regret.

Regarding coronavirus, some of these fears may be misplaced. If someone questions your decision to send your young, healthy child to school because of your child's risk of coronavirus and getting sick, while we don't have certainty that is not a fear well supported by evidence. If others question your decision out of concern for your health as a parent particularly if you have cancer or a heart condition, that concern may be well-justified. Our brains are wired to overly consider rare threats and under-imagine potential benefits.

You as a parent know your children and your family in a way that no one else does. Many times people love you and have their own strong opinions about the choices you make. When someone questions your decision, remind yourself that they don't have all the facts. When others make different decisions for their family, remind yourself that they are answering a different question.

We second-guess our own decisions and this is natural. Sometimes the worry, uncertainty and guilt that follow a decision are clues that we should reconsider. Writing this has me rethinking that trampoline — it's on thin ice. But many times these emotions are also manifestations of our love and concern for our children. The decisions feel so important to us because we care so greatly for our children.

You have made difficult choices about your family's health and safety already - whether about vaccination, safe sleep or carseats. Pediatricians help parents make these kinds of decisions all the time. Other more everyday decisions parents make also carry real risk — driving while tired or distracted or selecting other activities like skiing or soccer. You can make difficult decisions and, in the process of coping with the pandemic, maybe you'll learn more about what's important to your family.

Let's dive into how different activities will involve different levels of exposure. This knowledge will help prepare you for these decisions.

Exposures to coronavirus

While we are itching to resume our normal lives, coronavirus isn't over. Understanding the risks of your exposure is critical. Your personal exposure depends on both the community level of virus circulating and the number of other people you exchange germs with on a regular basis.

You do not control the level of virus in your community. This inconvenient truth can be so frustrating when you are doing the right thing, but your community isn't seeing improvements due to others 'choices.

To understand your local transmission, I recommend finding a reliable source of data you can follow over time. Directly checking the numbers once a week can give you an accurate sense of what's happening in your community with potentially less stress than following the local news. One option is a national dataset like the Mathematica model, where you enter your zip code and it generates a local transmission risk score based on currently available case numbers. Some local health departments are providing other dashboards that provide highly relevant information.

When picking a number to follow, many people ask which numbers are most helpful to track. If you look at deaths and hospitalizations from coronavirus, these numbers are the most objective and correct. However, they lag behind when infections begin surging by at least two weeks, so you should consider following other numbers as well.

If you look at the percent of tests in your community that are positive, that can be useful, but you also have to have a sense of how the quantity of testing is changing over time. As things open, many businesses, schools, and camps are implementing routine testing. Of course, people obtaining testing this way are less likely to be positive. In other places, clinicians have run out of testing supplies and are reserving testing for those who are most sick. This context can be more difficult to understand, but certainly lower percent positive test results are reassuring. This implies that your community has sufficient testing capacity and that overall fewer people are sick.

Now, as you consider your exposure to germs, you have more control over how many people you see and whether you mask or distance from them. The basic thing to remember is the primary spread of coronavirus is via droplets from other people. Airborne spread is less likely but may be possible, particularly when people are very sick and coughing, singing or shouting. Spread by touching infected fomites and then touching your face is also possible but less likely.

Keeping this in mind, the outdoors and good ventilation are important ways to reduced transmission. Fixed indoor crowds like bars or performances will lead to increased transmission. The Texas Medical Association published an infogram ranking the risk of various activities that is very helpful.[41] I have developed a similar chart with focus on children and family activities. Before we take a look, please note this is my best guess and my opinion. There are safer and riskier ways to approach each activity and in my ranking I've assumed you're taking precautions to make the activities as safe as possible.

KID'S EXPOSURES RANKED

LOW RISK

-Running, Tennis, Biking, Golf, Skiing

-Indoor appointments or shopping with a mask / Beach

-Playground / Outdoor play small group of kids <10

-Eating outdoors / Travel by car / Swimming, Baseball

MODERATE RISK

-School for kids < 10 / Eating indoors

-School for kids > 10 / Gymnastics, Volleyball, Dance

-Indoor choir or band practice / Travel by plane / Soccer

-Amusement park / Football, Basketball

HIGH RISK

-Large events / Wrestling

KELLY FRADIN MD @ADVICEIGIVEMYFRIENDS

When considering an activity, there are risks and benefits to consider. There are risks to you, risks to your loved ones and risks to your community to consider. The risk to you is relatively straightforward — you could catch coronavirus from someone else. The second section of my book was designed to help you understand this risk. If you are healthy and young, you may not be so scared of getting sick. I do not think you are incorrect in your assessment. If a member of your household is part of a higher risk group — such as infants, a pregnant woman or age over 50, or someone with chronic medical conditions — you may choose to be more cautious. Please remember the fact is that, with coronavirus, adults are higher risk than children. I urge you to remember and prioritize protecting your own health as a parent, not just the health of your children.

The risk to your loved ones outside your household is also essential to understand. Once you are exposed, it's very hard to know if you could be an asymptomatic carrier of COVID-19 or if you could be in the presymptomatic period. Once you are "in the mix" and more exposed, if you are seeing loved ones who are less risk-tolerant, protecting them requires substantial effort.

The most foolproof way to protect them is a 14-day period of isolation before a visit. This isn't feasible for most people to do electively. Some public health groups may recommend a seven-day quarantine followed by testing as a way to know you have decreased this risk. Testing after a period of isolation is preferable to testing before because, as we discussed earlier, it takes a few days following exposure to test positive if you've been infected. The alternative, once you are exposed, is to see higher-risk loved ones only in a distanced manner, such as waving from across the street or going on a hike together wearing masks.

Finally, the risk to society is one we may under-appreciate. Every case has the potential to infect others. The many places you may venture, such as the grocery store, pharmacy, gym, restaurant, your workplace, school or daycare. It's even possible that person you don't meet who rides behind you on the elevator or in the cab following you may be exposed to your germs, particularly if you are sick. So it's important to remember that we are part of a community and the fewer people who get sick, the fewer people will die.

Now that we've discussed the risks, it's worth discussing the benefits. There are real benefits to all the things we want to do. Some benefits are social — seeing friends and loved ones who we've interacted with only through a screen. These interactions are valuable and add meaning to our lives. Social contact decreases our likelihood of mental health problems like depression or anxiety. Many people have been bored during their time at home and the mental challenge of being out and about can be reinvigorating. There are logistical demands — people who have to move or assist in caregiving responsibilities. Health appointments I view as integral. It's worth reflecting on your big-picture priorities. What activities are most important to you and your family? Once you have your priorities in order, then you can prioritize your activities.

Additionally, you can think of ways to mitigate the risk. Maybe you've decided getting a haircut at a salon is out because it's too risky and not important to you, but if you can find someone to cut your hair outdoors and wear a mask, you can feel comfortable. An example with kids might be to say sports are really important to your family for health, friendships and fun. Basketball and gymnastics may be irrevocably high-risk for you this year, but it might be a great time to try biking or tennis, and these alternatives can serve the same goals in a safer fashion.

Some people find it helpful to have a breakdown of overall exposure. You can think about your entire family's direct and indirect exposure with rough numbers.

- **Level 0**
  - fully locked down, not leaving your home and getting things delivered. Family-only exposure.
- **Level 1**
  - leaving for grocery store / mandatory errands with precautions. Still hopefully family-only exposure, but maybe seeing a few people with precautions and still very low risk.
- **Level 2**
  - leaving home for work regularly, using nanny, virtual school. When seeing others, mostly taking precautions to mask, distance, or choose outdoor options. Still small exposure. Maybe instead of direct exposure only to your family, you are exposed to 5-10 people outside your family in close contact. Your indirect exposure to their close contacts may add up to around 20 people.
- **Level 3**
  - leaving home to engage in higher exposure work, children in daycare/camp/school, permitting optional activities and socializing more with precautions. Your family's direct exposure may be around 25-50 people. Your indirect exposure in this case will expose you to more, maybe 50-150.
- **Level 4**
  - If you aren't taking precautions or making attempts to decrease risk, you'll have the most exposure and the specific numbers will vary depending on your lifestyle.

Thinking of your overall level of exposure, not just individual decisions, can automate your decisions and reduce your stress. "We just aren't doing that right now." Your overall level of exposure can also be helpful when it comes to seeing others —

such as before a playdate, saying "we're a three," could give the other family the chance to consider the risk of seeing you.

When calculating your exposure, what matters is the *cumulative* exposure. If you are mostly level 1, but one day do a level 3 activity, that doesn't mean there is no point to being more cautious the next day. Imagine we put one person sick with COVID-19 in a box with a healthy person. Certainly the longer they spend together, the higher the risk to the healthy person because the exposure adds up over time.

It's tempting for some people to fall into "all or nothing" thinking and say that, since I had to go to the emergency room for that kidney stone, why bother wearing masks because I'm already exposed. It is true that when it comes to protecting a high-risk individual, you're either "clean" or potentially "dirty," but when it comes to your risk of catching COVID-19, you will still lower your risk if you continue wearing masks.

There's also a tendency to relax precautions over time when you feel things are going well. When communities open up or schools reopen, the risk is probably quite low in the first few days. As people mix more, the true risk of viral exposure may be higher just at the time when people feel more comfortable and perhaps slack off on their adherence to precautions. Maintaining your commitment and motivation to take precautions until a vaccine is available will be important.

TRAVEL

Many people have questions about travel — it's such a fun and functional part of our lives. When considering your travel plans, you have to consider the same layers of concern — the risk to you, the risk to your loved ones, and the risk to the broader community.

Regarding the risk of exposure, I'd like to clarify that airplanes aren't the worst spaces. Contrary to common beliefs, they do not recycle the air; medical-grade air filters are used. However, on an airplane, you are confined to your seat, often not physically distanced from others for the duration of your flight.

We cannot control others 'choices or guess their exposure. Maybe the considerate people near you are very diligent about distancing and mask on the flight. Maybe the person near you doesn't "believe in" masking and tested positive for coronavirus in the morning, but wants to fly to their destination to more comfortably quarantine there.[42]

With driving, you still have an exposure risk, such as stopping for food or to use a public restroom. But you remain in control of your exposure in a way that you don't on an airplane.

The community risk of travel is particularly important. In hindsight, had we limited domestic travel earlier in the pandemic, we may have protected many parts of our country from exposure to coronavirus. Tracking specific viral signatures, scientists have shown that virus originating in New York City led to more than 60% of cases.[43] While we hope that the CDC will keep us updated about which locations are high risk, and states will provide isolation requirements for people coming from high-risk places, in the U.S. we don't enforce these requirements. But we each bear significant responsibility for understanding how our actions could impact others.

We don't make decisions in a bubble

One really common issue is that we don't make decisions alone. It would be so much easier if only your opinion mattered and no one else's, but it's just not reality. You may fundamentally disagree with your co-parent about what the risks are, the benefits are and what's important. What should you do when this happens?

First, rely on what's worked for you in the past with disagreements. Every family has its own way of working through problems. Take some deep breaths and thinking as objectively as possible can help. Before you discuss the decisions, acknowledge where your opinions are coming from. Are you desperate for more help with your kids or to get out of your house? Are you really scared about your health or the health of loved ones? Acknowledge the emotions and try to focus on the facts when making these decisions.

I've seen with my friends and family that these decisions immediately become quite heated and morally fraught. Because of the nature of the pandemic and the associated risk of life and limb, it's no surprise that emotions run high. But it's worth remembering that, when trying to work through these things with people you love, whether they are more conservative or more liberal than you are with regards to the risk, you have common ground.

Best practices for communication include using a lot of I statements. So in your conversations you may use statements like "I am very scared about ..." or "I am feeling very burned out ..." or "I am very worried that..." Then you may consider the other person's perspective and repeat it back to them to be sure you understand. "I hear that you think this would be a good idea because..." Then look for common ground: "I see we are both focused on the kids, but I am worried about their social development and mental health and you are worried about the risk of MIS-C." Once you get to this point, often the best thing to do is both step back, sleep on it and come back to it another time.

When you readdress it, if you know where the other person is coming from, you can present evidence about why you think they are mistaken and continue to negotiate. Or you can look for other ways to compromise or mitigate the risk of whichever decision you are struggling with.

Sometimes you might reach a dead end. You may find that your loved one cannot be persuaded to behave in a way that makes you feel safe. This can bring about a lot of difficult feelings – anger, sadness, and guilt. If you've been able to communicate your opinions and feelings but are still stuck, there may not be much other to do than hope your loved one changes their mind and wait for the vaccine.

When dealing with shared custody and two families, these decisions and conversations get even more difficult. At the bottom of it, we all try to make the best decisions we can for the child. In most situations, that means finding a way to preserve and promote relationships with both parents. The original custody plan may make less sense now that someone has more space, better internet access or a different work schedule. If you decide to renegotiate and keep the child's needs and well-being at the center of the discussion, I think you'll figure it out.

Decisions about childcare

Worries about childcare have overwhelmed parents during this time. For those of us who work — or used to — we structured our lives around providers who helped us care for our most beloved children. And then the shutdown happened and we were on our own.

By now, maybe you've made your decision about childcare, but if not, let's examine it. First, do you need help with your kids? Most people do in some capacity. Many people can get by without it for a while, but when it comes to a longer period of time, it's not what they would choose.

When approaching this decision, it's particularly easy to consider the risk of exposure and stop. I would encourage you not to stop prematurely, but to go on and explore the risks of not having help and the benefits of having help. As parents, when we are doing our best, we don't want to think about how it is not quite enough. The reality is that, for many parents, trying to work, cook, clean and mind the children full time can be less than ideal. I don't say this to invoke guilt, but rather to release it. Our expectations of ourselves can be unrealistic.

There is a real risk to not having help. I worry about the safety of children with parents overstretched and in fact there's a whole chapter about this later on. Might you fall asleep holding a baby or while driving? I've talked about my concerns about your mental health. If you are struggling — like many right now; it's OK to be struggling — the risk of continuing on without childcare may harm you. And your children depend on you.

The benefits of childcare can be enormous. When children have a caregiver whose job is to look after them, often that person can focus on giving a child more attention and support. When you have more bandwidth, you can enrich your child's development and education consistently. If your childcare options allow for exposure to other children, that may be really wonderful, particularly if your child has been lonely or missing opportunities to play.

As we consider the risks and benefits, obviously they vary depending on what route of childcare you'll take. A disclaimer — I've had two kids and chosen two different routes of childcare. With my first, I was working nearly 60 hours a week and needed flexible scheduling to make morning rounds at the hospital an hour away and hired a nanny. While a nanny was great at helping around the house and seemed perfect for a baby, when the child got older, I didn't like having a nanny so much.

I was piecing together storytimes, playdates, and sports classes and trying to be her boss and make sure we were on the same page about development and discipline and nutrition. I found managing a nanny to be a lot of work. Perhaps I had the wrong nanny for me or, as a nervous first-time mom, I didn't trust and delegate as effectively as I should.

With my second, I was working less and found an excellent daycare with a topnotch curriculum and incredible teachers. The social engagement provided in the infant room astounded me. My child was really benefiting from being around other children all day and getting tons of extra stimulation. She didn't seem to be sick more than my son had, although surely she brought home some daycare colds.

For many people, a nanny is simply out of consideration due to the cost. I want to address up front that many parents who have to work and don't have the option may feel a lot of guilt and concern about the exposure risk of daycare.

Daycare will involve other families and giving up the feeling of control over your family's exposure. However, daycares can and will do a lot to become safer — they can implement more intensive healthcare screenings, more hand washing, reduce unnecessary adults in the building, promote masking in some groups and cohort the children. Many of these interventions are similar to the ones being implemented in schools, which I'll discuss soon — evidence-based and likely to effectively decrease risk. Daycares have safety rules imposed, government standards to adhere to and a leader who enforces those standards. From what we've seen thus far, young children are less likely to catch and spread coronavirus. Remember those children with cancer who didn't catch coronavirus from their infected parents? Physiology seems to be on our side as the youngest kids have fewer receptors for the virus and likely emit droplets with less force.

Despite these facts, it's possible for viruses to be passed in a daycare setting. Children can get and spread coronavirus and when you have a decent number of children with a few adults in the same room all day interacting, if one is sick there will be virus present. The exposure risk in these settings is also affected by community transmission of the virus. If your daycare is taking precautions and your community transmission is low to moderate, it's likely that sending your child to daycare will be fine.

For those who have the option of nanny or daycare, consider what you would have chosen pre-pandemic and why. If you felt strongly about your choice, it may still be the correct one. Direct comparison of the exposure risk between a nanny and daycare skews in favor of a nanny.

Certainly, considering your exposure from a nanny depends on a lot of factors. Who is your nanny? What is his or her daily life like? How will your nanny commute? How will your nanny handle physical distancing and masking outside of work? How will the other people in your nanny's household affect your exposure?

Keep in mind that you can't micromanage someone's life outside of their job — it's not kind. Depending on your local laws, it may be illegal to ask about off-duty conduct. Be careful to develop a thoughtful policy about sick-days. You wouldn't want your policies to encourage your nanny to come to work if he or she isn't feeling well. Hopefully you have a respectful relationship with your nanny that facilitates open communication. This will help integrate your nanny into the team of people raising your child and improve your confidence working together during this time.

When a new person enters your home, washing hands, leaving shoes by the door and even changing clothes may be helpful ways to decrease the likelihood of bringing virus in. Parents will have to decide whether to include their nanny in their family pod or to ask a nanny to mask and distance either from adults or children. I'd encourage you to use some of the shared decision-making tools I've discussed with your nanny. Certainly his or her input is important.

Now, once your nanny is at work, imagine how the day with your child will go. Will they mostly stay home or will they be out and about to playgrounds and playdates with other children? Staying home with parents working from home can make separation more difficult for children. The choices about what the day will look like matter. If the nanny plan involves six different families with whom they will interact without precautions, the exposure risk of the nanny may be similar to, if not greater than, daycare.

Since we know that adult-to-child and adult-to-adult transmission is higher, having a playdate with six adults and six kids represents a higher risk than nine kids and three adults. I'll talk more about playdates later on.

I can't say whether daycare or a nanny might be the right fit for your family. It depends on your risk tolerance, finances, and the specific people you trust your children with. In general, easy answers aren't accurate. When someone says, oh, of course a nanny is better during a pandemic, the truth is much more complex. It depends on the nanny, the plan and the alternative.

Should schools reopen? How?

School is a child's world. Developmentally, sending a child off to school is a big step. Their world expands outside that of their family. There is a new social hierarchy and friends. School fosters emotional growth and development and essential learning. School is so much more than just childcare.

As a society, we have to prioritize it and find ways to make it acceptably safe for students, families and teachers. This involves substantial fundraising for sanitizer, equipment, smaller class sizes, and more buses. Even with the implementation of ideal precautions, we have to understand that bringing individuals together during a pandemic carries some risk.

Countries ahead of us opening schools and case tracking have seen dozens of sick cases and tested hundreds of exposed students and staff and found low transmission rates in the context of low numbers of coronavirus cases in the community.[44] In Australia, the early numbers were as low as 3/1000 exposed people in schools getting coronavirus, though this was in settings where efforts were made to decrease transmission and attendance in schools was low.[45] More recently, a high-quality study out of Korea confirmed this finding that children under 10 seem less likely to transmit coronavirus at home or in school settings.[46]

Certainly, even if children are lower risk for transmission as they seem to be, no one is claiming that children have no risk for transmission. Children over 10 may transmit disease as frequently as adults. Children are at school with adults, and adults connect and collaborate in their management of the school day as well.

We have to balance the risks of infection with the real benefits of school. Schooling at home is not a real viable option for many families who need to work to maintain a roof over their heads and keep food on their plates. Alternative childcare arrangements may be worse for transmission, with fewer safety checks and less consistent cohorting.

The academic declines we have seen over the first portion of lockdown have been startling.[47] Not only are children dropping out of school, but children's learning has stalled. Engaging through technology requires a lot of focus that some children do not yet have developmentally. The rich learning environment of most classrooms doesn't translate perfectly to being online and can require parental support that isn't feasible for some families.

Additionally, core services provided by schools — such as speech therapy, physical therapy and occupational therapy — are medically necessary and sometimes not provided outside of these environments. Schools have transitioned to becoming the medical homes in many communities with primary care, dentistry, vision services and mental health services rolled in. School closures decrease children's access to these resources.

Unfortunately, many of these problems with remote schooling hit vulnerable students with special needs or from low-income families the hardest. In most areas, private schools have more funding and flexibility to change practices. Private schools may be able to adapt to new regulations more quickly and completely than public schools, which will worsen disparities. Even within public schools, we are seeing some parents choose to withdraw their children for the consistency of a smaller pod of children sharing a private teacher. While these withdrawals may help keep class sizes small, they may also lead to decreased funding for public schools.

Private schools and childcare centers may not withstand the closures economically. Eventually this pandemic will pass; either a vaccine will be delivered or everyone will get it, and we'll want our institutions available for childcare in the future. While all of these tough issues warrant debate, discussion and careful planning by public health and government officials, as parents we have decisions to make.

We are all used to protecting our kids, but we should view coronavirus through the lens of how do we let kids live their lives safely without risking the health of our communities and our families. When facing your decision about your child's education, I think it's important to separate "should schools open" from the decision of "should I send my child." Emily Oster's decision making framework I referenced earlier reminds us that the more specific the question, the easier it will be to find the answer. This is absolutely true, and phrasing the question more specifically will help you. For example, I can't answer "Should my son go to school?" But I stand a chance at answering "Should I remote-school my son while working part-time from home, or should I send him to his school where they are taking all the recommended precautions seriously?"

Regarding interventions to reduce the spread of coronavirus in school environments, we don't have a lot of evidence to fall back on about which are the most important. So we have to use our understanding of coronavirus transmission and principles of infection control to make our best guesses.

We know that individuals infected with coronavirus are often asymptomatic. This important fact means that, as we select our plans for schools, we are faced with assuming asymptomatic or presymptomatic children and teachers will carry coronavirus into school. As we've seen in other countries, the risk of spreading it seems low, but many of these countries have tried variable interventions.

In my opinion, the most important intervention is to cohort children. Coronavirus is a sneaky beast. As many as 90% of children testing positive for coronavirus will be asymptomatic and potentially infectious. There is an inevitable and intrinsic lag in our ability to identify children who have been exposed. Knowing who is and who isn't carrying the virus will be next to impossible.

We have considered interventions to decrease the number of students and staff with coronavirus who enter school. Temperature screening is a very popular idea, but has some fundamental flaws. Even when we look at children sick with coronavirus who come to the emergency room, only just over half have a temperature of more than 99.5F. Technically, 99.5F is not even a fever, so if we exclude students who have that temperature, we will cost their families time at work, doctors visits, and testing, but we'll also miss as many as 95% of the students who have coronavirus entering school.[48]

If temperature screening had no risk, surely it would be worth it to identify even one unexpected fever, but there are risks. Thermal scanners that are contact-free do not seem accurate enough to be useful, nor are they available and scalable to be included in every school.

This leaves us with mostly temporal/forehead no-touch thermometers that require someone — a teacher or nurse — to get close to every student. Even wearing a mask, this may be a contact for transmission. Bottlenecks while waiting for temperature checks may cause adults and students to mingle, crossing cohorts. If the temperature checker is sick with coronavirus, he or she may infect a lot of people.

Testing for active infection prior to school also seems like a tempting intervention. Even with a good test, tests have costs and flaws. Let's imagine a scenario of testing implementation. We plan to open our hypothetical school with 1,000 students in an area where community spread of coronavirus is low, for example 1%. Assume we have access and resources to use a very good test that is highly sensitive, picking up 95% of cases, and highly specific, correctly identifying 95% of people who don't have disease. It's likely that, of the individuals who test positive for coronavirus, only 11% will actually have it. The other nearly 90% will have to go back to the doctor for testing and miss school. Testing also will miss any children who may be exposed and yet to mount sufficient virus to test positive. Also worth considering is the exposure risk of swabbing all those students, the cost and protective apparel required.

Screening questionnaires for parents to complete daily about exposure risks and symptoms seem like a good idea. I worry as a parent these quickly become automated. I can't imagine in my typical morning rush out of the house stopping to consider a symptom I hadn't already thought of while clicking the boxes. Skeptics say that parents may still give a dose of ibuprofen for a fever and send the child to school — these aren't foolproof. But many school districts will choose to adopt these, whether by an app or a Google sheet. When done responsibly, respectful of privacy and varying levels of literacy among parents, there is little harm — only the cost of time and implementation.

So temperature screening, testing, and screening questionnaires have their limitations. We're left assuming everyone entering school may have coronavirus. So, limiting the spread of illness to fewer people is essential to protect students, families, teachers and other school professionals.

Cohorting correctly is very difficult. Before you even get to school, busing introduces a mix in the cohorting. Special courses such as science lab, math enrichment, art, and music often involve mixing groups of people. Children typically have eaten out of the classroom in cafeterias. Afterschool, sports, and extracurriculars are other risks without obvious solutions. In middle and high schools, children typically change classes. Teachers often share a lounge for meals or rotate in and out of classes. Cohorting requires reimagining the school day and reconsidering class size.

When you cohort really well, if a child develops coronavirus and exposes a class, the class will need to shut down for a 14-day period of isolation, but the rest of the school can safely remain open. As we inch toward wintertime, this is important. If schools are unable to cohort children effectively, they will have to take other precautions more seriously, such as masking and physical distancing. And once a positive case is identified, a larger percentage of the school will need to be shut down.

Speaking of precautions, a fundamental one I haven't mentioned is handwashing. Historically, most children have not washed their hands at school at all, despite toileting and eating. I have been in a lot of schools and often there is not enough soap, paper towels, hand sanitizer, or sinks available to really facilitate frequent and effective handwashing. What is available is all too frequently provided by generous school staff members, rather than school budgets.

Time is another obstacle to handwashing. Children need to be given structured opportunities to clean their hands when they arrive, before and after they eat or use the restroom, and before they go home. Hopefully handwashing access will improve with coronavirus, but undoubtedly this oversight has worsened prior cold and flu seasons.

While handwashing may seem so basic, we touch our faces every few minutes. If you have an infected material on your hand, you can introduce that into your eyes, nose or mouth and become sick. While evidence suggests that droplet transmission (inhaling droplets with coronavirus on them) is the primary method of infection, handwashing will decrease risk of contracting coronavirus.

Another critical way to decrease transmission substantially is masking. Masks aren't perfect. Cloth masks seem to block as much as 95% of outgoing germs and approximately 70% of incoming germs. In other words, if a coronavirus-carrying teacher wears one, it will reduce the droplets she puts out with coronavirus by 95%, which is pretty great. However, if she is the only person in the classroom wearing a mask, it will block 70% of the incoming germs, leaving her relatively exposed.

This means that, to be very effective, everyone needs to mask, including students. Masking effectively will be very difficult for our youngest learners or children with developmental impairments or sensory issues. There is a risk that masking will make it harder for children with hearing impairments to learn and may decrease comprehension even among those with normal hearing. I have concerns about whether social and emotional learning will be impacted, particularly for young children. However imperfect, masking is likely the most important intervention to decrease transmission within pods.

Another factor that will affect transmission within classrooms is ventilation. How frequently the air is exchanged, the humidity and temperature of the air, and the filtration system will modify the likelihood of transmission. Outdoor classrooms and open windows have been suggested to improve these factors, but in many places truly modifying or improving school HVAC is costly and slow.[49]

All of these options have to be considered within the specific context of the school and community. The age groups of the students determine the risk of transmission as well as the child's ability to responsibly wear a mask. The needs and preferences of the teachers should be accommodated. The barriers to cohorting and physical distancing should also be considered. It would be so much easier for everyone if we could have clear instructions for exactly what will work, but we have to proceed with trust that, given the options, our local officials and schools are doing the best they can to implement comprehensive policies effectively.

Likely the single biggest factor driving whether schools experience outbreaks is community spread of coronavirus. Consider a state where 1-2% of the individuals tested are positive and substantial testing is in place. The likelihood of an infected student bringing coronavirus into the school is low — say 1 out of our 1,000-child school (0.1%). Given the lower risk of transmission of children and the precautions to further reduce that risk, the likelihood is that this may lead to one school-acquired case and one classroom shutdown.

Consider a state where 20% of tests are positive. Certainly, most people tested obtain testing for a reason, either symptoms or exposure, and hopefully students walking through the door of the school don't have those risk factors. But when community prevalence is high, the rate of children entering school will be high as well. So imagine the 20% test-positive state has 2% of children who show up at school carrying coronavirus. Assuming the same risk of transmission with our precautions in place, this would translate to many more school-acquired cases; maybe 20 sick children would expose 20 classrooms and each cause one case. That translates to 2% of your school getting sick.

Also, when community prevalence is high, the likelihood of an infected teacher is also higher. Infected teachers are highly likely to spread more coronavirus than infected students, based on our current understanding. Adults have been linked to most "super-spreader" type events, such as in Westchester County in New York, where a man spread coronavirus to as many as 170 people, or the distanced choir practice in Washington state that infected 87% of attendees.[50] Many adults interact in the school day, from bus drivers and teachers to parents at drop-off. Taking steps to protect the adults in schools is essential. We can decrease adult-adult interactions, require masking, and provide safe spaces for teachers in school.

All of this said, where do I stand on the plans to return to school? I have many concerns. Foremost, I worry about the inequalities in access to education during this time. It's not fair that some of our poorest and most disadvantaged children, many of whom are children of color, will have more limited access to high-quality instruction during this time. Addressing this is an urgent priority and not easy, particularly given limitations in budgets and busing. The Johns Hopkins e-School+ initiative provides robust insights into all of the considerations at play and I encourage you to read what they've written.[51]

I am also concerned that hybrid models are setting up students and parents for failure. While mixing virtual learning with in-person learning will provide some in-person instruction to more students, it may increase community transmission, as students may mix more outside of school. Children respond really well to a routine and a few days virtual and a few days in-person will mean many children are in a state of constant adaptation.

Because of these issues, if I were in charge, I would have prioritized school access for those with the most barriers to virtual learning — including disadvantaged students and students with special education needs. Then I would prioritize in-person learning for younger students, those under 10 who are at lower risk for severe outcomes from coronavirus, transmit coronavirus less frequently, and have the most difficulty with virtual instruction. Certainly, all of our school leaders are doing their best to make the best decisions for their school communities.

All of this said, most of this discussion is about things you can't control as a parent. The point of diving into all this is to give your decision some context. Schools will offer a range of strategies to protect their students and, after reading this, you'll have a sense of where your school lies.

Should my child go back to school?

Once you have the specific plan from your school, you can really dig into your question, "Should I send my child to this school taking these precautions in my community with its current (high or low) prevalence of infection" or "Should I homeschool/virtual school and maintain our family's isolation at my preferred level." I tried to put the direct health risks of coronavirus in context by age and risk factor earlier in this book, so by now you have a sense of those. Some of you may have very high-risk people to protect and that may make for an easier decision. For many, it's worth thinking through the risks and benefits thoroughly. While everyone's situation will vary, I think it's likely many people fall into a few thinking traps.

The first thinking trap is that virtual school will carry less risk of exposure to coronavirus. This depends on *how* you carry out your plan at home. What will the whole of your family's life look like if you go to school or pursue virtual school?

If both parents work from home and virtual school will mean not seeing anyone or seeing a small group of similarly restrictive families, you may indeed be decreasing your contact from school.

This may be necessary and the smartest thing for families at high risk.

However, if by pursuing virtual school you are piecing together childcare with a few different caregivers and families, these exposures can add up over time. Imagine with a bigger family and a desire to keep your children engaged socially with others or in important extracurriculars, you may find your contacts quickly add up. If you have three kids who each see three kids regularly and attend one sports program each, your family is exposed likely to nearly 100 families a week. If your children attend school and each have a class of 20 children with sports and socialization inside of the school day and not much happening outside, I can imagine a scenario where you are exposed to fewer than 100 families a week.

Also, your school will have safety parameters that you may or may not have outside of school. Another consideration is that physical school might change parents 'exposure. If your children go to physical school, you may choose to see more people or go to work in ways that you couldn't otherwise, which may lead to more direct exposures.

Who is exposed also matters. We've seen from some data mentioned previously that children may transmit coronavirus less than other adults. So while indirect exposures matter — your child may bring home germs from others — those risks are blunted by the chance that your child will not always get you sick. Though it varies by age, some data have shown that children under 10 transmitted coronavirus to only 5% of their household contacts. Infected older children were more likely to transmit similarly to infected adults in the range of 18%. [52]

I mention this again because it's worth considering the direct exposures and indirect exposures for the highest-risk people in your home, who are likely to be adults. If your kids go to school and you mostly work from home, as a parent your direct contact with others may be much less than if you are physically helping facilitate playdates and sports to enrich virtual school.

Along these lines, parents often fall into the thinking trap of considering themselves martyrs to their children. But as we think about what is best for your children, please remember to prioritize your needs as a parent. For some, myself included, we are headed for burnout if we don't get our kids back to structured programs. The logistics or necessity of childcare are drivers for many in this decision.

In the scenario with virtual school plus playdates and extracurriculars, most of your child's needs are handled by a parent and a parent has direct ability to manage the risks. This sense of control can feel really helpful. You are choosing the families, the context for interactions, the playdate activities and sports. But with this control and this power comes a lot of responsibility and work. Worry-work takes up a lot of time and energy and managing a household of people at home is a big commitment for a parent.

The next thinking trap may be that what you are used to — likely in-person school —will be best for your child. By now you probably know how your child handles virtual school. I know many students who have thrived with virtual school. In some households, there are fewer distractions at home and more flexibility to spend time on subjects that need more attention. Other children were difficult to keep on task at home and the stress of this eroded the parent-child relationship.

The virtual school to which you are returning may be different from the one you experienced in the spring of 2020. Schools have been working hard all summer to get up to speed on improving their virtual curriculums. If you had a bumpy transition in the spring, it's quite possible it could be better in the fall with more comprehensive teacher training, resources, and preparation on your part.

Consider your goals for your child as different seasons of childhood have different priorities. Is your child struggling to stay on track and really needs all the academic enrichment he can get? Is this a time when fundamental skills are being established, such as learning to read or basic math skills that you can or can't help with? When your child is struggling with learning disabilities or academically behind, there are two ways to think about what's best. Either you think personal attention you can provide at home will help or professional help from school will make the biggest difference. For other children who are gifted or who learn easily, promoting their social skills and providing regular opportunities to see other children may be the No. 1 goal of school.

As we consider social development, which plan will support this need best? It's easy to assume in-person school will be best because of the structure and more children, but the reality of the school to which our children are returning may not as socially enriching as the school we are accustomed to. Depending on your school's plan, there may be less group work and fewer tactile experiences with our peers this year. Virtual school may leave more time and bandwidth for enriching social experiences, depending on whether you have a large family or close friends you plan to continue to see regularly.

Yet another consideration is your child's physical health. Consider how your child will move their body (or not) in each scenario. Again, you have to keep in mind that athletic programs may be reduced, given our new normal.

It would be so much easier if there was one obvious best solution for everyone. But the truth is I can't tell you what's best for your family. You have all the tools to decide. So you decide. Commit to it and don't look back.

Optimizing virtual school

At this point it seems likely that at least part of the school year will be virtual for many students. Even if you start in person, you may end up quarantined for weeks or shut down in a surge. So it's worth considering what can we do to improve virtual schooling.

ACKNOWLEDGE LIMITATIONS

Years before distance learning started, as a mom I enjoyed teaching my son to read and helping him to acquire new math skills. I loved seeing him learn and finding ways to facilitate it. However, I never imagined I would bear such a responsibility for his education. While I know a lot about development and have read a lot about curriculums and best practices in schools, I am not a teacher. I have immense respect for the work our teachers do. Many parents feel the pressure of supervising remote school and feel overwhelmed. At the outset we have to acknowledge our limitations. We are not skilled and experienced educators, and our teachers and schools are still available to guide us and provide incredible resources for educating our children. I can support my children's learning at home, but by remembering my role is to support and not take over, I can take a bit of the weight off my shoulders.

When it comes to the youngest learners, caregivers will require the most support. Many of the fundamental skills kids learn in preschool and early elementary years don't translate well to virtual instruction. Children this age need a lot of hands-on experiences associated with their learning — part of their curriculum is handwriting and scissor use, for example. So much of the benefit of these years is on developing foundational friendships and learning how to participate in a classroom.

Certainly parents have homeschooled and found ways to provide exceptional educational environments for young learners. Nearly universally, homeschooling parents have chosen to do this, have a caregiver well prepared to homeschool and have access to homeschooling co-ops and extracurricular activities to enhance social and emotional growth outside of the household.

So to expect parents to crisis-school at home and reach similar outcomes, particularly if they are working or watching other small kids, is unrealistic. It's developmentally unrealistic to expect children to learn as well virtually and independently, particularly when so young. So what does this mean?

For children under third grade, parents have little choice but to ask for help. Whether you can find a buddy family to collaborate with, hire a tutor or babysitter, or take the time away from other responsibilities, devoting more resources to schooling these youngsters is going to be necessary. However, I realize this is difficult or impossible for many families, so in the end we have to do our best.

If your child isn't meeting your educational goals because you don't have the time or the skills to offer the support necessary, I would try not to worry. Children are resilient and in most cases can catch up quickly. Many education advocates encourage play-based learning over direct instruction in the early years.[53]

While children often spend eight hours at school, the recommended time commitment for homeschool is much less. The Illinois State Board of Education suggested the following for the core curriculum with additions of optional work and enrichment.[54] I am including this to give you an opportunity to make sure your expectations are developmentally appropriate.

Grade	Minimum	Maximum	Sustained attention
Pre-K	20 minutes	60 minutes	3-5 minutes
K	30 minutes	90 minutes	3-5 minutes
1-2	45 minutes	90 minutes	5-10 minutes
3-4	60 minutes	120 minutes	10-15 minutes
6-8	15 min/class/day 90 min/day	30 min/class/day 180 min/day	1 subject area
9-12	20 min/class/day 120 min/day	45 min/class/day 270 minutes/day	1 subject area

PRIORITIZE GOALS

When resources for education are strained, selecting your goals is essential. We have fallen into remote schooling rather precipitously, but it's worth wondering: Does the virtual instruction plan make sense for my child? We may not have the bandwidth to check every box every day and make the most of every Zoom session.

But, as we consider our educational plan over a week or a month, we can decide if we want to focus on reading, writing and math or if we'd like to devote more time and energy to other special classes, like science, social studies or music. It's worth considering your child's preferences here too, especially for older learners. If you take the time to write out your goals for your child's school year and pick the most important two or three, you can prioritize those on days when time and energy are limited.

We spent years planning and selecting the right school for our children, and now change happened so quickly some parents and kids did not have the right fit. Some families struggled with virtual school not because of intrinsic difficulties with remote education, but because of the fact that the offerings didn't fit their interests and needs.

For example, my school put a lot of effort into offering remote physical education, and it was very thoughtful, well done and cute to see kindergartners doing pushups together over Zoom. For the first month we made it work; my son would participate enthusiastically, provided I did it with him. But after a while we both began to dread it.

Instead of fighting about it, I chose to pivot. I remembered my underlying goal here and the school's goal was to encourage my son to stay active and promote his fitness. So I said as long as my son chose a fitness activity every day, he could skip it. I said his teachers also said it was OK, but I did not ask permission. We hope to cultivate long-lasting good habits, so it was important to me that he enjoy the time he spent moving his body, whether by tag, bike-riding or nature hikes.

All of this to say sometimes it's OK to say no when something isn't working. Leaving some empty space in your child's day can provide opportunities to relax, play, read, create, build or connect — all developmentally enriching in their own way.

Conversely, it may be a good time to add something. Some days, particularly dreary winter days when we couldn't go outside, we would explore new learning content online, whether trying to learn typing, watching a YouTube arts and crafts video together, or doing our first coding projects.

These activities were high interest for my son and educational. I thought of these as electives in his day of enrichment. So when his interest in them waned, we would move on to something else. I think adding something of high interest has a lot of promise for teens as well, and I'll include a few ideas in the resources section at the back of the book.

GET INTO A GROOVE

When my son started kindergarten, the teacher sent the clear message that the first six weeks are about setting classroom expectations and routines; the learning will come. As families adjust to their new schedules, remember that this phase-in period is an important opportunity to set yourself up for success. Organizing your space and training children to manage as much of their responsibilities as possible will take time and effort, but hopefully will pay off in helping maximize their independence.

Telling yourself that the routine will become easier and more natural and setting your expectations low the first few weeks may avoid unnecessary drama. Give yourself and your children time to adjust to new routines.

In the first weeks of the pandemic, color-coded schedules circulated on the internet. I have to admit some made me roll my eyes and some filled me with rage (or was it envy?). "Schedule hate" seems to be a thing, but of course different approaches will work best for different families. At the least, having a predictable rhythm to your day, if not a full-blown schedule, is critical to your success.

A routine is typically simpler and more flexible than a schedule. My family, with our 2- and 6-year-old children, fell into a routine of play, breakfast, and independent work, including Zoom meetings for my kindergartner, and outdoor play. Then we would have lunch, the baby would nap, and I would work with my kindergartner. After the baby woke up, we'd enjoy outdoor playtime again before dinner. Mostly I fit my work in whenever my children were occupied or my husband available — often after bedtime.

This is the routine that worked for us and is nothing magical. Notably, I am the primary caregiving parent — a choice that was intentional for us, but just one of the many options available. Some families may have more balanced arrangements by choice or necessity. Sometimes much more elaborate back-and-forth schedules are required to make it work.

Almost undoubtedly, the most important part of your schedule is bedtime. Good quality sleep will make your little students ' schooldays go so much more smoothly. Regular sleep and wake times are a core of sleep hygiene. Other ways to promote good quality sleep include limiting screentime before bed, as the specific light frequencies in screens are known to make it harder both to fall asleep and stay asleep. In older children, monitoring caffeine consumption and keeping screens out of the bedroom may help too. I've put a couple of resources for improving your children's sleep at the end of the book.

FAMILY MEETINGS

Family meetings are a great parenting tool. Not only are they opportunities to connect with your children, but they are opportunities to demonstrate listening and negotiation skills. Group problem-solving and talking through frustrations are instructive for children who over time will internalize and mimic the way you think about challenges.

Bruce Feiler discusses how families can implement business best-practices to improve their family life in his best-selling book *The Secrets of Happy Families*. He makes a strong argument for family meetings. While it's daunting to introduce a new practice during an already challenging time, I think now is the moment for family meetings.

When you implement family meetings, you a have a chance to review the weekly schedule, logistics and any important updates. But it also gives you a chance to check in with your family. How are they feeling? How is schooling going? What are the goals for the coming week?

Young children may not be developmentally prepared for these discussions, but can learn a lot by listening. Before you expect older children to engage productively, you'll have to demonstrate willingness to open up about your life too. It's helpful for children to hear "I am stretched thin this week because I have a big deadline Tuesday. So while I can't play basketball on Monday, I'd love to find a time on Wednesday to do something special with you."

Also helpful for children to hear is "I haven't been able to exercise as much this week as I would have liked. Exercising makes me feel better and is so good for my health, so this week my goal is to exercise at least three times." Being open allows your children to participate in your goals. "Can you remind me later this week that I said this?" "Can you help me exercise more by going for a bike ride with me?" "Can you work on your Lego by the Peloton so I can watch you while I exercise?" You are showing your children that you prioritize self-care; you can set goals and make plans to improve yourself.

Another layer of learning on this topic is failure. Some parents may be hesitant to share their goals with their children because we all know that the children *will* remember and potentially nag you about it. However, showing children that you can set a hard goal and potentially fail at it and keep trying without falling apart is an important lesson and an opportunity to learn about a growth mindset.

Besides just individual progress and goals, family meetings provide opportunities for collaboration. "I had trouble concentrating on my math homework because my sister kept interrupting me." "But I was bored and I wanted to play with you." Children, given an opportunity to talk through problems like this and brainstorm solutions, may surprise you when they come up with good ideas — and ones you might not have thought of.

Keeping kids safe during coronavirus

One of the things I worry about most is the unanticipated fallout from this pandemic. With children in unexpected places with distracted parents (myself included), as a pediatrician, I worry about safety. No one wants an unnecessary ER trip during a pandemic, so let's review the basics of childproofing for young children.

When thinking about your plan, spaces where your child will be unsupervised are the most important to consider. In a playroom or their bedroom, we must assume they will do their worst to cause mischief and these should be triple-checked for safety. In kitchens, bathrooms and laundry rooms, hopefully young children will be supervised, but you still need to consider the worst-case scenario and plan to prevent accidents.

All over the house, accessible power outlets should be covered. Furniture such as changing tables, dressers, and bookcases should be wall-mounted. Televisions, mirrors and heavy pictures should also be secured. This requires some power tools and is labor-intensive, but is so important. Blind cords can be a choking and strangulation risk and should be out of reach or secured using a tensioner device.

Cleaning products should be out of reach, including sprays and dishwasher and laundry pods. If you have any medication, including vitamins and over-the-counter drugs, the medication should be kept up high and preferably not in a bathroom where the heat and humidity can damage medication over time. In the kitchen, it's worth establishing the habit to cook on the back burner and ensure that knives are out of reach. Kitchens should be stocked with a fire extinguisher.

If you have a pool or access to water, you should know it takes only a moment for a child to drown. I strongly recommend a multilayer water-safety plan, including alarms for the door, fences with childproof gates and swim lessons. With each of these alone, there is the potential for failure, but the more layers to your plan, the more protected your child.

I have heard that a lot of gun stores have sold their stock, as people are scared of civil unrest. Particularly if you are a new gun owner, please be sure than any guns in places where children visit are locked away with ammunition stored separately.

Children are having unprecedented screentime, but remember that screens are also child safety risks. People can manipulate and bully children easily on screens. Children can also bully others easily and can make undeletable mistakes.

If you have a young child, if possible use "guided access" functions to keep kids on whatever task is designated or stay in the same room to make sure they aren't finding ways to get into trouble (or get scared). With older children, consider a monitoring plan such as Bark or Circle. Common Sense Media is a great resource to help you navigate the waters of internet safety.

Pediatricians are highly attuned to the fact that domestic violence increases during times of chaos, stress, and confinement at home. In fact, nearly every holiday season, domestic violence hotline calls increase, attributed partially to increased financial strain and substance use. Almost certainly there is more domestic violence during this pandemic. If this is affecting you or someone you love, please seek help and know it's not your fault. Even during a pandemic there are ways to get out of a toxic situation and people who can help you. You are never alone. Call 1−800−799−SAFE(7233) for a national 24/7 hotline.

While most of this is also important during regular life, I think we can all use a checkup for our household safety these days.

Speaking with children about coronavirus

We are all learning as we go when it comes to communicating with children about coronavirus. Before getting into details of the content of what we say to children, I'd like to consider the quantity.

Many of us are consuming a lot of media about coronavirus — including this book. As a parent and a pediatrician, at times I've felt strange talking about anything else, since it's all we're thinking about. But talking about coronavirus constantly in front of our kids may make them more anxious. Even when you try to reduce the load of coronavirus conversations, there are unavoidable exposures to things like radio advertisements, which right now are all about sanitizing services. Be mindful of how much coronavirus content your children are digesting.

Given that I've been so focused professionally and personally on the news, you might be surprised that I made the mistake of speaking to my children about the pandemic too little. All of a sudden, we were almost a month into Zoom schooling with no return to school planned, and I hadn't really said much about it to my kids. Really, this was to protect myself; I was having a tough time with all the changes and uncertainty and I worried that I couldn't cope with their worries on top of mine. My husband brought it to my attention and helped me address it.

Giving your child space to share what they know, and what they are thinking about, is important. Really listening to what's on their mind is also instructive for you as a parent to see what level they are at in their understanding. Often children have been exposed to more than we imagine, and they have big gaps and the only way to know what your children understand (and don't) is to ask.

I'm going to provide a few examples of ways you might check in with different age kids.

- **My 2.5-year-old.** "Oh, honey, things have been a little different recently. Do you remember when you were going to school every day with your teacher? Do you know why we aren't going to school right now? I hope we can go back to school soon. Is there anything you miss about school?"

- **My 6-year-old.** "Our lives are so different than they were a few months ago. Do you have any questions about what's been going on with the virus?

- **Eleven-year-old.** In my experience, tweens are best approached when you are side to side, not face to face. When driving or walking somewhere, "How have your friends been coping with the virus?"

- **Sixteen-year-old.** "If you were in charge of school reopening, what would you do differently?"

When considering the content of what you say to your child, I recommend you prioritize being honest, calm, reassuring and empowering. If your children ask you questions and you don't know the answer, admit it. If they ask questions that make you uncomfortable, such as about deaths, I would encourage you to be honest but try to spin difficult truths back to reassuring facts. For example, "Yes, a lot of people have died, which is why we are all taking this so seriously and doing our best to protect the people we love from getting sick" or "yes, people have died, but mostly it's been people who were at higher risk to get sick; luckily, you and your sister are healthy and if you get the virus you'll likely be fine."

It can be difficult to be calm when you are very stressed. If your children want to talk about coronavirus at a time when you don't think you can do it well, you can make an excuse. "Oh, great question, honey; let me think about that and finish making lunch and then we can talk about it." Then, if you need to, you can go hide in the pantry, take a few deep breaths and call your friend. Another way to be reassuring is to acknowledge difficulties and provide unconditional support. "I can tell you are worried about coronavirus, and I am too. I'm glad we can talk about it and be worried together."

For everyone, even adults, spinning worries into action can be helpful. "Yes, I really miss your grandma too. Do you think we should send her a card?" "Our community is having a lot of virus going around now, which is why we have to wash our hands really well and wear our mask the whole time we are out."

Like talking to your child about anything important, choosing the right time is essential. Imagine your boss coming into your office for a big discussion and interrupting you and how that would go over. Play is the work of children and if they are busy doing something, they won't be as open or forthcoming. It may be easier for a child to have a weekly small conversation than a monthly big one, depending on your child. Check-ins can also be included in family meetings if you do them.

Life in a pandemic can be so overwhelming, we are at risk for getting too caught up in the news. Please remember to talk to your children about other things too, such as the books, movies and games they are enjoying. Doing things together as a family — whether hikes, chores, or home improvement projects — can be a welcome break from feeling stuck in Groundhog Day repetition of life at home during a pandemic.

How to get your kid to wear a mask

<hr/>

Cloth masks aren't perfect. But they are the best way for us to resume normal life without risking the health of our communities. They definitely work to decrease emission of droplets carrying coronavirus and are pretty effective at blocking inhalation of others 'droplets too. With good cooperation from our communities, mask-wearing could stop the exponential spread of coronavirus.[55] Masks are part of the solution; hand hygiene and distancing are essential components too.

We have to embrace masks as we re-enter society. A lot of people don't like masks. Maybe they are hot or a nuisance, but they are not dangerous. When you reframe masks as the key to resuming more "normal" life, suddenly masks seems a lot more positive. Your branding and attitude toward masks will be very key to how your children perceive masks.

People are *really* scared. Individuals in our communities have real risk factors or love people with real risk factors. These individuals see the statistics and worry about death. There is only so much they can control to decrease their risk, which makes it even more stressful. Some of our neighbors, classmates, and coworkers desperately need us to mask.

Masks are not for children under 2. Children who cannot remove a mask on their own developmentally may not be safe to wear one. Some children and adults with special needs may be unable to wear a mask for this reason.

Introducing a new habit to a child can take time. For many children, learning to brush teeth effectively can take years and adopting a mask is a similar skill, but we don't have years. First we have to make a mask seem familiar and safe.

We can familiarize kids to masks by:

- Decorating a mask.

- Playing a mask-wearing game.

- Putting a mask on a stuffed animal.

- Taping paper masks on photos or drawings.

Once your child can successfully tolerate a mask for a few seconds, you can provide positive feedback and slowly, over time, your child may tolerate the mask for longer periods. It can also be helpful to use activities your child enjoys as carrots. Practice short outings to the doughnut shop, the bookstore or the playground when your child will wear a mask and use the natural consequence of if you can't wear the mask, we can't go.

With older teens, getting them to wear a mask may require more sophisticated maneuvers. Hopefully their peers will also wear masks, as peers are so important to our teens. Maybe teens can be convinced to wear matching masks or decorate masks together.

Motivational interviewing is a counseling technique I use a lot with families; it is evidence-based and respectful. It may come in handy here and in the long run save you some time, fights, and frustration.

Ordering your teen to mask may backfire. First, determine where they stand on masks. They may be pre-contemplative and not really open to using them. For these teens, giving third-party materials and asking them to learn why you think it's important can be helpful. If they are OK with the idea of masking but not really doing it yet, in the contemplative stage, learning what barriers to masking exist can be very helpful. Is it that they feel awkward or stigma against masking? If so, you can target your counseling to those issues more specifically than mask-wearing in general. If they are in the preparation stage, they are planning to mask and may need help with logistics — choosing a mask, planning when to wear it and how to clean it. Once they are successfully masking, you may have to work on maintenance. We know over time that healthy behaviors decline — diets and exercise plans notoriously fall off track. So if you have child who is successfully masking in appropriate situations, providing positive reinforcement and continued mask motivation can be important. At this stage, some teens may feel motivated to encourage their peers to also mask, and this is a way to self-actualize and really make lemonade out of lemons.

Some mask logistics: The outside of a mask is dirty and covered with respiratory secretions. So it is likely to be contaminated, potentially even with coronavirus. It's important for children and adults to avoid touching the mask often. Each time the mask is touched, the hands should be washed. The mask should be removed by holding the straps and placed either into the laundry or into a "dirty bag" headed that way. To make this work, most people will need multiple masks to make it through a day.

We are all going to have to be empathetic to those around us and not shame others when we don't know their full story. Wearing your mask should protect you some from others unable to wear their masks.

Social skills during a pandemic

Everyone has wondered: Isn't this social isolation bad for kids? Yes. Undoubtedly. Loneliness was a public health concern prior to the pandemic, as it's been linked with increased adverse health outcomes. In children prior to the pandemic, we knew that lonely children are at higher risk for depression, poor sleep, worse executive functioning and poorer overall health. We know from other pandemics that the isolation from lockdown can cause long-lasting effects on mental health. Schools and activities provide so much social exposure for kids, how can children function without it?

Before we panic too much, we should remember that children are remarkably resilient. And it's worth remembering that you as a parent are an important anchor to their social network. Even if your circle has shrunk considerably, there can still be many rich opportunities to find meaning and connection within your pod.

How can we encourage continued social skill development while we are at home? We are physically distanced but not socially distanced. How does this work in practice? Some kids can express a need for social connection, and I worry less about these kids who may seek out their own social outlets. It's the kids for whom social connection doesn't come easily that I think need the most attention during this time.

Some simple ideas for promoting social interaction include:

Board games	Encourage language skills, negotiating taking turns and following rules, and coping with disappointments.
Games without boards	Charades, Eye Spy, a story chain, drawing or building games, scrabble and chess can be facilitated over video chat or using apps.
Meals	While traditionally accomplished in person, virtual meals can facilitate connection.
Alternative methods of communication	Writing letters, leaving surprise scribble stones or putting a stuffed animal in a window are examples of other ways kids can send messages while having fun.
Parallel virtual play	Going on a virtual field trip "together" or participating in a YouTube art class together can provide a common goal.

Remember that you provide essential social exposure to your kids too. Sometimes we coexist with our family, but taking the time to really connect and listen every day is important. Conversation starters at family meals can be helpful, either ones you find for free by Googling or card kits you can purchase, such as Table Topics. Rose and thorn is a classic way to share the best and worst part of your day. Cooking together and doing chores can be a way to reduce the burdens on parents and encourage activities to encourage social skills and practical life skills too.

For younger children, setting up an "invitation to play," doing a science project or a building challenge can foster collaboration and planning ahead. These activities can make old materials such as blocks or magnatiles seem new again and encourage small kids to use a new vocabulary.

Books are great for social skills. In almost every book, there are emotions to label and relationships to explore. Books about "Bucket Filling" can encourage children to think about giving back to their loved ones, families and communities. "The Invisible String" is another classic that talks about how we are all connected, even when we are far apart. I've included a list of my favorites in the resources in the back of the book.

If you are a new homeschooler, it may be worth considering alongside the reading, writing and arithmetic that a social and emotional curriculum is a huge part of an effective education plan. Making time for some exercises to encourage children to gain skills in these domains can really pay dividends in terms of helping them have healthy relationships, become more independent and be more pleasant to interact with.

Self-awareness and self-management skills refer to knowing yourself, identifying your emotions, and knowing what that means for you. I've listed some activities here for children of all ages, I started with ones more compatible for younger learners and ended with some teens may enjoy.

- Trace everyone in the family and add descriptor words about what makes each person unique.

- Label emotions in picture books. Ask what the angry or sad character could do to cope.

- Teaching and practice buddy breathing. The child lies on the back with a stuffed animal on his or her stomach and then takes deep breaths to allow the "buddy" to go up and down. Box breathing is another variant of breathing practice — you breathe in for a count of four, hold the breath for a count of four, breathe out for a count of four, and hold your lungs empty for a count of four.

- Yoga and meditation can promote mindfulness, well-being and improve sleep quality.

- Use the letters of their name to create words expressing your personal traits (for example, maybe Thomas is thoughtful-helpful-original-meticulous-active-silly).

- Taking a personality quiz such as Myers-Briggs may encourage children to learn about themselves.

Another category of social and emotional learning includes social awareness, interpersonal skills, and positive relationship maintenance. We can promote this by labeling interpersonal issues that we see in books or movies and brainstorming other ways to respond. Writing letters to loved ones can foster the ability to empathize and consider what the recipient would want to read. Kids can put on a puppet show with a conflict, write a story or record a movie.

The last domain of most social and emotional learning plans includes demonstrating decision-making skills. Contributing to the family household can practice these skills. When children master new chores like washing cars, folding laundry, or organizing toys, they use new skills. Older kids can engage in family debates about topics and learn from switching sides. Families can have achievable, specific goals and work together toward them, such as starting a garden or improving in a sport.

Social and emotional learning has been a buzzword recently for good reason. Helping your children develop these skills has always been worthwhile. The stress of the pandemic makes these efforts more important than ever.

Managing stress

I spoke earlier about how during this pandemic adults are at risk for mental health difficulties, and I want to give you a few more tips for helping cope with the high levels of stress we're facing.

When I first went to the store after months of isolation, wearing my mask, it felt very strange. My friend asked, "Are you nervous about getting coronavirus?" I am not. I am masked, washing my hands, and taking precautions. And if I get coronavirus, I am low-risk. I will almost certainly be fine. But for me, anxiety comes with adjusting to the new normal.

I want to be a good neighbor and keep others safe and comfortable. I am not yet familiar with the new rules at the grocery store. How does the restaurant handle takeout orders? I am nervous about making a mistake or offending someone as I navigate things.

When it's just me as an adult, it's one thing. I can take my time and hold my own against other adults. But as I start to bring my young kids out and about, masked and respecting physical distancing, I feel more concerned. I worry about my children violating physical distancing or masking rules in a way that makes someone else feel uncomfortable or unsafe.

I'd equate to the nerves I felt when my son transitioned to riding his scooter the eight blocks to preschool in Manhattan. In some ways, the stakes were high. A quick misjudgment on his part could truly hurt someone, whether he barreled into a street full-speed and got hit by a car, or swerved too close to an elderly individual using a cane and caused that person to fall.

Similarly now, with coronavirus, the stakes are high. But just as it took time for him to learn scooter etiquette, it will take time and practice for all of us to develop a fluency at interacting with our environment in pandemic times.

I have found myself repeating these mantras to myself. I hope they help you too.

- We haven't mastered the mask yet, but we're learning.

- I know we might make mistakes, but that doesn't mean we'll get sick.

- It feels strange because it's new and we haven't done it in a while.

- I am afraid of making someone else feel uncomfortable, but my family is doing our best.

- Just because it feels strange doesn't mean it's the wrong decision.

My approach to resuming normal life after a pandemic is founded in a growth mindset. While a growth mindset has been encouraged to help children with academics, it was originally a concept learned from successful adults. Carol Dweck, in her book *Mindset: The New Psychology of Success,* dug into how people with a growth mindset have perseverance and resilience that can help them overcome life's setbacks. I would consider this pandemic for most of us the ultimate setback. But motivational mantras like "I can learn from tough times" or "I can do difficult things" can help carry us through as parents.

IN KIDS

While you may be feeling anxious going out as a parent, we also need to consider your child's mental state in resuming normal life and discuss fear of going out. Luckily, many children will bounce back into outings as allowed. But some will struggle with the process.

Undoubtedly, the attitude and stress we bring to this will affect our children. Before you start changing your practices, give your kids an optimistic, fact-based update. "Our doctors and leaders have started reopening our community because we have the virus more under control. We still have to be careful and we will have to do things differently, but this is great news and I am excited to X,Y,Z."

When kids ask about something specific that is unclear, be honest! "I don't know about in-person school, vacations, or when we'll see Grandma, but we will keep you updated when we have more information." Expect that they will circle back again and again to discuss the things most important to them; try to be empathetic and remain consistent.

It's very easy to debate different activities and discuss the risks and benefits in front of your children. Even if they are playing in the same room or in the backseat of the car, often they are listening. When you can, try to hold these conversations in private. It is overwhelming and upsetting for kids to discuss what's not allowed often. For children, considering the risks of outings/activities extensively will decrease the enjoyment and benefit. As parents, we can carry the weight of our decisions. The constant hum of concern and fear about coronavirus can be exhausting for us as parents and also for our children. Certainly, mature tweens and teens can and should be more a part of the discussion.

Once you decide something is OK, set realistic, clear and enforceable limits. For example, "we can go on a bike ride together, but stay at least a bike's distance away." Discuss rules in advance; send a clear and confident message that this activity is allowed and OK. Check in about your anxiety level and take some breaths before the activity. If your kids express fear, normalize it! "We haven't done this in a while; I am not surprised it feels funny!" Remind your children of any rules as needed during the activity and try not to change the rules on the fly or set developmentally unrealistic expectations (2-year-olds will touch each other).

If you have concerns about the decisions being made in your community, before sharing these with children and venting about it, consider how it might impact them. If you are really anti-masking in school or camp, for example, your child may have more difficulty getting on board with it if it's expected.

Our children have an uncanny ability to sense when something is wrong no matter how hard we work to shield them from the news. Luckily, children are incredibly resilient. I wouldn't assume your child is suffering unless you see evidence. And if you do see signs of stress affecting your child, don't panic. Stress can be an opportunity to learn coping skills and grow. Help is available when stress and anxiety become overwhelming.

Signs your child is stressed:
- Sleep disturbance, excessive sleep

- Potty training setback

- Poor appetite

- Clingier than normal

- More tantrums

- New fears of the dark or the dog

- Shorter attention span

- Worse academic performance

- Physical complaints (e.g., stomach pains)

If you see signs of stress, please don't feel guilty. This is an incredibly stressful time and it's natural for a child to struggle. Struggling and learning to cope can promote resilience.

Approaching things head on doesn't always work with young kids, so I do not recommend asking leading questions (such as, "Are you worried about the virus"). They may be concerned about something you'd never imagine. For example, on lockdown, my son's main concern was not having access to a specific book where we were staying.

If you do learn your child is stressed, resist the natural urge to dismiss your child's feelings. Doing so may reduce their likelihood of sharing their feelings in the future. It's also important not to lie. While it's easier in the moment to say "I'm sure school will be open and everything will go back to normal soon," it may not be accurate. Your child needs to trust you.

Focus on the routine. Children thrive with a routine, structure and predictability. This can help during periods of unrest, but at the same time it can feel impossible to provide consistency when things are so up in the air. By prioritizing the structure of your child's day — the meals, wake and sleep times — your child can feel more secure.

Poor sleep is one of the most underrated causes of anxiety. It's well known that sleep deprivation will induce clinically significant levels of anxiety. It has to do with the stress hormones induced by failing to rest. They trigger a high arousal state and can cause you to be hyper-vigilant and have trouble relaxing and sleeping. Sleep hygiene, limiting screentime before bed, and maintaining consistent sleep and wake times and a quiet, dark environment can make a big difference. When trying to improve sleep habits, extra soothing before bed rituals — such as an extra book, a massage with lotion, an extra story snuggling in the dark, or practicing with a breathing buddy — can help. Importantly, there are medical reasons some children and adults have poor sleep, so it's worth reaching out to your doctor for help if you are struggling with sleep.

With younger kids who may not be able to use language to convey their feelings, puppets, drawing, or storytelling can be ways to explore tough feelings. If your child latches on to a story with a character who feels scared or sad and wants the same story over and over, that may be a clue there is something to explore there.

Another reasonable coping mechanism is distraction. Some kids may need help selecting and getting started on a distracting project. A puzzle, Lego, crossword, baking project or craft can help a child find a sense of flow. When we are engaged in a task that is precisely the right level of difficulty, we can lose track of time. These moments can make us feel happier.

For those of you with older children, if your child is able to tell you their worries, this seems like it would make it easier. However, I think often helping older children cope with unfixable stressors can be even harder. As a parent, it's important to be a good listener. If your child can confide their stress in you, that is a powerful sign you have done something right and such a protective factor for your child's well-being. You want to do everything you can to validate their concerns, confirm their safety, redirect their energy constructively and maintain this open communication.

Finally, it's worth noting that children sometimes can seem anxious when in reality they are bored and restless. Telling one from the other can be difficult. Benign anxiety or situational anxiety can be a passing feeling, just like boredom or restlessness. If changing the situation helps, it should reassure you. For many, feelings of anxiety can be transient. However, when children day in and day out are struggling, please seek help.

Clinically significant anxiety is intense, excessive and persistent worry and fear about everyday situations. Anxiety was common before the coronavirus pandemic and now it's nearly standard. If your child seems to struggle with overwhelming anxiety, it may be time to ask for help.

Certainly, situational depression is also common in children during this time. You may see more obvious signs of depression in your children, like sadness, hopelessness or social withdrawal, but other symptoms can be more subtle and include the following.

- Irritability or anger

- Changes in appetite (high or low)

- Changes in sleep (excessive or insufficient)

- Difficulty concentrating, excessive fatigue

- Physical complaints like stomachaches or headaches that don't respond to treatment

If your child has several of these symptoms for longer than two weeks, please reach out to your pediatrician. If it hasn't been two weeks, but your child's symptoms are severe or concerning, don't hesitate to reach out. One of the first things a pediatrician can help with is screening your child for suicidal ideas. While it's upsetting to think about children with this degree of distress, it's not uncommon. Sometimes these thoughts can affect children at younger ages than you might expect. Children, and adults for that matter, can have these distressing thoughts and hide them – until we ask we can't be sure. Pediatrician, psychiatrists, and mental health professionals have training to help children who experience these thoughts.

Many people still hold stigma against seeking mental health care. The No. 1 reason I hear is fear of medication. I always tell my patients, "You're a doctor who has already done an evaluation, made a diagnosis and formulated a treatment plan and decided that's the only option?" This is not how seeking care works.

Pediatricians, family medicine physicians, psychiatrists and psychotherapists have extensive training on performing thorough evaluations and helping diagnose problems. Once an assessment is made, then we can counsel about treatment options. Before we even make a mental health diagnosis, we have to exclude medical problems – for example obstructive sleep apnea can cause poor quality sleep and many problems regulating emotions. If there is concern for a mental health diagnosis such as anxiety or depression, treatment options often include behavior modifications and therapies — in fact, one of the most evidence-based treatments is cognitive behavioral therapy.

When it comes to our health and the health of our loved ones, we don't always see things clearly. A doctor offers a different perspective and adds valuable input. Keep an open mind and don't hesitate to ask for help.

Returning to sports after coronavirus

Sports are wonderful opportunities for kids to be physically active and socialize with friends. Athletic teams are really important to many children. We are all eager to get kids back to play safely as soon as possible.

Deciding when and how to reintroduce your child's favorite sport can be tricky. First, I'd like to remind you that pre-participation exams or sports physicals are always a good idea. Some states, given difficulties in accessing physicians during lockdown, have made these doctor's visits optional, much to the consternation of pediatricians.

Most commonly, a child can have a pre-participation exam at the same time as their annual checkup with the pediatrician. The first part of the exam includes a thorough history. We may ask about prior concussions, injuries, allergies, medical conditions that may interfere with sports, and symptoms like dizziness, chest pain or shortness of breath. In older girls, we take a menstrual history.

During the exam, pediatricians check a lot of things, including the heart, lungs, vision, abdomen, hernias, joints (for hypermobility), strength and flexibility. Mental health assessment in athletes is also important — athletes can suffer from performance anxiety as well as generalized anxiety and depression. Some sports can place pressure on making weight that can lead to eating disorders.

Once the doctor has all the information, they can counsel you about ways to stay safe while participating. We can help you consider what sort of gear should you use and how to prevent overuse injury. For children with disabilities, we can talk about how to find opportunities that might be the best fit. A family history of sudden death, fainting with exercise, congenital heart disease, and abnormal heart rate and rhythm are indicators that might prompt referral to a cardiologist.

All this is to explain and emphasize that, before the pandemic, pre-participation exams were important because of the screening and counseling. Infection with coronavirus has been shown to cause damage in the hearts of adults. 25% of adults hospitalized with coronavirus have cardiac injury. Viral inflammation of the heart can cause thinning of the heart wall or predispose to arrhythmias. MIS-C may cause abnormalities in the coronary arteries that supply the blood and oxygen to the muscles of the heart. We don't have any data yet on the risk of heart damage to children who have coronavirus, but in children whose infections do not require hospitalization, we expect it to be low. However, identifying cardiac problems before resuming competitive sports is necessary — making these exams more important than ever.

The current recommendations for heart screening after coronavirus infection before returning to sports are targeted toward adults. It's likely that these will be updated in the months to come, so check with your pediatrician. In young or recreational athletes, most children who have mild or moderate coronavirus symptoms can resume play without issue after a full recovery. Serious competitive athletes without symptoms who test positive for coronavirus should consider a two-week rest period followed by a slow reintroduction of activity. Competitive athletes who have moderate symptoms should see a physician before resuming play to consider cardiac testing. A child hospitalized for coronavirus should have a cardiac assessment during their hospitalization and a plan for follow-up if needed.

These pre-participation exams can be an opportunity to discuss which sports are safest for exposure. As with any activities, there is a spectrum of risk to consider. Some activities can promote athletic skills with next to no risk — drills that you can do alone or fully distanced. Working with your team broadens your circle of exposure, competing against other teams enlarges it, and traveling to play poses additional risk for spreading virus between communities.

Some ways to make sports safer include sanitizing hands before play and not sharing equipment. Switching out the balls can decrease transmission of fomites (particles on balls), but remember most people get sick by breathing in other people's droplets, so breathing heavily right next to someone else is concerning. Practices outdoors or in well-ventilated spaces are safer. If the sport has to be indoors, masking or reducing the density of players may help decrease transmission risk. Some sports require contact between players; when possible, limiting this to only when necessary (for instance, during games, not practices) would decrease risk.

Intrinsically, some sports like tennis, golf, track, baseball and swimming are easier to do safely. Dance, volleyball, basketball and soccer require closer contact and may be more difficult. Wrestling seems impossible to do safely.

With each sport, we also need to consider the logistics. With swimming or ice hockey, for example, many children change in small areas which could serve as nidus for transmission. Adults mixing at drop-off or gathered to watch games may add to the risk of transmission. We should protect the health of our coaches as we do with teachers. This is the right thing to do, and if a coach is involved with multiple teams, he or she may be at risk of infecting many people.

We should remember that choirs, orchestras and marching bands — non-sport extracurriculars — may also be high-risk activities for transmission. Coronavirus has infected all of our activities.

With sports, as with other decisions like childcare and schools, we have to return to your individual decision. How important is the sport to your child? What are the alternatives? How can you alter the activity to maximize the benefit and decrease the risk? We also have to consider the context — what is the risk level of your family should you get sick and what is the current level of community transmission?

Doing routine things during a pandemic

Of course, when families are making such drastic efforts to reduce their exposure, it's natural that we think critically about each choice and routine medical and dental visits are not exempt from this. I would like to remind you that the doctors and nurses, therapists, and special education professionals you or your child may interact with should be very aware of how important it is to prevent the spread of the virus. I have heard of many doctors being shunned and even having others in their household shunned as many presume the risk to be higher among this group. Data from the peak of the epidemic in New York suggests otherwise.

Health professionals working on coronavirus units had lower rates of coronavirus infection than others in the community.[56] Is it because health professionals were more adherent to the physical distancing, masking, and hand hygiene recommendations? Maybe. Is it because people who work in healthcare have had very high exposure to other strains of coronavirus and had innate and cell-mediated immunity block infection with the new strain? Possibly. But don't assume that all professionals are higher risk, because they may not be.

Let's review why these routine visits are still important.

THE DENTIST

Should I take my child to the dentist? As a pediatrician, I have utmost respect for dentists who see children. Not only do dentists have lot of patience and incredible bedside manner, they have incredible technical skills that can have a tremendous impact on children's quality of life. Most parents underestimate the importance of oral health.

Childhood dental caries (cavities) is the most common pediatric health problem. Cavities cause pain, difficulty speaking, worsen nutrition, impair sleep and decrease quality of life. Poor dental health has been linked all sorts of bad health outcomes in adults, including worsening glycemic control in type 2 diabetes, strokes and heart attacks.

Knowing this, I strongly recommend that you keep your children on a schedule of oral health exams and dental visits. I know you may be scared about someone getting close enough to clean their teeth, but you should be aware that dentists know how to keep both your child and the rest of your family safe. If dentists were common vectors for disease transmission, they would not be able to work all winter because of the common respiratory infections that circulate.

I was dismayed when some newspapers reported that going to the dentist may be high-risk. Certainly dentists may vary in how they choose to interpret precautions — ask to learn more about their policies before you go. Most dentists in my area are using N95 face masks and shields and sanitizing all their equipment. Dental offices were already well ventilated. Dentists have also changed policies to request that parents wait outside and have altered their schedules to provide less crowding. For most people, the risk of poor oral hygiene or untreated dental cavities is worse than the tiny risk of catching coronavirus at the dentist.

THE PEDIATRICIAN

Should you go to the doctor? One of the best things to come out of the pandemic is increased insurance reimbursement to provide telemedicine services. There are some situations where telemedicine works seamlessly. If you're worried about mental health issues, trying to improve diabetes or obesity, or following up about chronic asthma, virtual visits can be a great solution.

But sometimes in pediatrics we need to lay hands on your children. Kids can't reliably tell us what's wrong and we need to perform an exam. For example, ear pain is one of the most common complaints.

History alone is a terrible way to guess whether a child has an ear infection. Most ear pain relates to sinus pressure, but it may be referred pain from a tooth problem, a bug in the ear, an inner ear infection, an outer ear infection (aka swimmer's ear) or other rare pathology. Other common complaints, like cough or abdominal pain, can be very difficult to handle over video.

Well visits carry important benefits for children's health. I can't include a list of every scary thing that's been caught early at a well visit because it would be longer than this book! But I can give you an example. Once I had a 15-year-old boy at a physical who really didn't want a genital exam. This is a tricky topic, as it's his body and as a pediatrician I have to respect it. At the time I was lucky enough to have an available male colleague to offer to do the exam, but still my patient refused. He wanted a clearance for sports and we reached a dead-end; I felt I couldn't provide it without a full exam.

I did a psychosocial screening, wondering if there was trauma, but I wasn't getting anywhere. Then finally I sent in the social worker to see if he'd open up. Whether it was her charm or wearing him out, my social worker convinced him to tell me he had a problem "down there". It was a swelling and it turned out to be cancer. He had been embarrassed and hadn't told anyone, but we were able to get him prompt treatment and he did fine.

But it just serves to remind you that we do these exams for a reason. In babies, the most common things that come up are growth issues. Just so we're clear, these are important — when children don't grow well, their brain is also not growing well. Or in some cases we catch a large head circumference and learn their brain is under pressure from too much fluid. Congenital heart disease, hip dysplasia and jaundice are other things we screen for in early visits, which are critical.

In older children, we often catch diabetes and leukemia before a child ends up critically ill. In teens, at times it seems like every week one presents with a crisis, whether it's suicidality, anorexia, or a sexually transmitted disease. Teenagers are excellent at hiding these things from their parents and it's not always the children you would imagine who have a problem (which is why we ask everyone).

Putting the critical things aside, we see children with vision and hearing impairments every day. Providing referrals for ophthalmologic assessment, glasses, hearing tests and otological interventions is essential to promote children's development and well-being. All to say, skipping a well child visit or an annual exam is not a good idea.

Vaccination rates have fallen with limited visits, clinics being closed and parents being scared to take their kids to the doctor. We've already passed a threshold that may pose a risk for children. Illnesses such as pertussis, measles and the flu require a high percentage of the population to be vaccinated to provide adequate protection.

The vaccines in the first six months of life protect against many infections, including some bacteria that almost certainly live on mom and dad. Common bacteria like Hemophilus influenza and Streptococcus pneumonia can cause severe illness in babies — problems like meningitis that can lead to lifelong disability. Delaying these vaccinations poses risk, even if you're keeping your children home. The AAP published strong recommendation even at the height of the outbreak in New York City that vaccinations under 2 should not be delayed. I agree with this assessment.

Pediatricians are motivated to keep you and your family healthy because they care about you. By now pediatricians should have comprehensive policies in place to protect you at visits. If you are worried, ask! Your doctor can explain what to do and why.

GIVING ALLERGENS

This is a minor point, but parents are always nervous giving little babies foods that can trigger allergies. During a pandemic, we are more worried with potentially limited access to the pediatrician and ER.

As a pediatrician, I know that if we all wait to introduce common allergens, food allergies will be more common. The only tool we have to prevent food allergies is to give the foods early, ideally between 4 and 6 months, and regularly. I would encourage you not to wait. Go ahead and give those foods as you would during normal times.

In case you aren't familiar with normal times yet, ask your pediatrician for advice. Typically we recommend that, if a first-degree relative (mom, dad or sibling) had a food allergy or if the child has persistent eczema, asthma or other food allergies, it's best to hold off until cleared by a doctor.

I would consider having diphenhydramine (common brand name Benadryl but generics are fine too) on hand first. Pre-pandemic, I didn't think it necessary, because this medication treats only non-emergency allergy symptoms like itch or rash. But for now, a quick trip to the pharmacy may be a bigger deal. Give the new foods for the first time in the morning or anytime other than right before bed.

If you see signs of a reaction, most commonly rash, call your doctor! Severe reactions are very unlikely for low-risk children on the first exposure. Vomiting, swelling of the mouth or lips, feeling dizzy or fainting, and cough or difficulty breathing are examples of reactions that would warrant emergency treatment. Please be sure to contact your pediatrician if you're worried about a reaction.

Where to go from here

I've given you a ton of advice. I've done the best I could in under a month to provide a helpful resource.

However, I worry I haven't met your expectations. We all have a deep desire for a solution to this struggle. I wish I could wave a magic wand and know the perfect thing to say to help you. But I can't fix this. No one can.

Reflecting on the pandemic has me thinking back to early April. On March 17th, my family was supposed to go on spring break, but our vacation was cancelled. Instead we went into lockdown as cases exploded in New York City. It was cold and we were cooped up without much to do.

To say I was stressed would be an understatement. I wasn't sleeping. I was checking my phone every fifteen minutes, panicked about the cases and deaths I knew were coming. I wasn't sure if my family would stay safe, or how I would get groceries. The sky was falling, and I was in full crisis mode.

My mom sent me a text message to check on me. My Instagram tag is @adviceigivemyfriends because my writing journey began with the idea of sharing pediatric and parenting advice with my friends. Her advice is worth sharing.

Friday April 3rd 9:58pm

Mom:

"Twenty years from now, you will have an empty nest.
You'll look back on this time as an amazing gift of
unstructured time with your family."

Me:

"It's really hard. My 2-year-old, 6-year-old and work all
need me in different ways at the same time."

Mom:

"Your kids are such great ages to relax and watch them
learn and develop reasoning skills. These skills take time
not always available in class."

Me:

[Not responding, feeling rage, stress, and emotions not
consistent with receiving an amazing gift]

Mom:

"You are doing a great job."

With all of the fear, stress and the uncertainty of this time, we
all have our moments when we feel overwhelmed. When we are
in the hole, it can be hard to look past this to have perspective.

But the pandemic will end. A vaccine will be available, and we
will move past this time. Life will go back to normal.

When the dust settles, what will your family remember about
these times? Will you laugh about how mom reorganized the
whole house? Will you cringe remembering the fighting about
social distancing or about remote schooling? Will your children
grow in unexpected ways, mastering laundry or cooking? Will the
relationships in your family blossom in the context of less
competition with outsiders? Will the slower pace of life with
fewer activities be something you choose to continue?

Even if there are more hard times than good, you will have learned something about yourself, your family, and what's important.

I don't know you, but I know you are doing your best for your children.

You were so concerned, you read my book. You have all the information, knowledge, and advice you need. You can do this.

You already are.

Appendix

Acknowledgements

I could never have written this book without the logistic and emotional support of my husband Bill. He's the best, and nobody beats him.

My independent, loving kids have been wonderful pandemic companions. They've also helped me refine many of the parenting techniques I share here.

Thanks to my dear friends Diana Gershuny, Laura Owen, Lyndsey Kruzer, and Victoria Kelly for encouraging this ambitious endeavor. Thanks also to my early readers who provided feedback: Mikey, Susan and Roger Fradin and Roy and Nona Fahl. My friend and colleague Dr. Kristina Malik provided invaluable insight into the sections relevant to complex care. As an OB-GYN, Dr. Amy Bednar helped me make sure my pregnancy chapters were accurate and provided helpful references.

My dear friend Ashley Zalta put me in touch with Angela Ledgerwood, a publishing pro who despite being a total stranger read my very raw work and gave me the confidence to charge ahead. Thanks to you both.

A big thanks to my Instagram family who keep me motivated by sharing your questions, stories and struggles. Dr. Hina Talib (@teenhealthdoc) has been an invaluable sounding board and support during this process. Dr. Pooja Lakshmin (@womensmentalhealthdoc) is an inspiration and helped me expand my audience. I wouldn't be here without Dr. Natalie

Crawford (@nataliecrawfordmd) and her podcast episode about why doctors should join Instagram. Dr. Sasha Shillcut (@becomebraveenough) and her StyleMD Facebook community have inspired me along my journey. Thanks to Dr. Dana Corriel (@drcorriel), the SoMeDocs, and my Insta-colleagues, all of these physicians out there sharing evidence-based information for good.

As a pediatrician, I've always loved Emily Oster's books *Cribsheet* and *Expecting Better*. They explore the data behind decisions relating to pregnancy and babyhood that I always like to share with my patients. She has been so kind by going live with me to chat about schools and by reading and helping to promote my book.

Social media may have risks for children, but for the purposes of communication with leaders in medicine, it's invaluable. The Facebook groups for pediatricians, school health doctors, and the Physician Mother's Group were invaluable resources as I tried to identify, interpret and synthesize all of the information available about coronavirus. It's a lot of work to moderate these groups so my thanks goes out to Dr. Karen Cress, Dr. Melissa Dhundale, and Dr. Hala Sabry.

Thanks to Tom Kearney for helping with last minute line edits and Victoria Black for the amazing cover.

Let's stay in touch

On Instagram, I've connected with thousands of families. While I counsel parents everyday on the dangers of social media, there's also beauty. Via social media, I've shared so much of the sort of practical advice I tell my friends. This advice is useful and bridges the gap between the pediatrician's office and your home. Physicals and office visits are short, and even the best doctor can't possible impart everything you need to know. So let me be your pediatrician's assistant. Reach out and let me know how you liked the book and let's connect. Join my newsletter so we can keep in touch should the details of the pandemic change.

@adviceigivemyfriends

Disclaimer

The information above is based on reliable publicly accessible sources, but due to the nature of a pandemic and study of a new disease subject to change over time.

I am a physician, but not your physician and this is educational information not medical advice specific to your children or your family. I strongly suggest you discuss your own decisions with your doctor who can give you tailored advice should your family be at increased risk for severe outcomes from coronavirus.

The views expressed here, on my website, and social media pages represent my opinion and not the opinion of any current or prior employers.

Resource list

I put together a comprehensive list of resources with hyperlinks that don't function in a paperback. If you'd like to pull it up on the computer, go to http://adviceigivemyfriends.com/paperback

RESOURCES ABOUT CORONAVIRUS

The CDC, the WHO and your state or local health authority are all great resources.

John Hopkins has a comprehensive data dashboard to see facts about coronavirus epidemiology.

The site Pandemics Explained will show you a locally derived risk index to say what community spread is like near you now.

This Mathematica tool synthesizes geographic case data and individual risk factors to give you ballpark, specific information based on recent research.

The CovKid Project is maintaining a dashboard with cases reported in children and has a lot of information and resources.

The Virtual Pediatric Systems (VPS) network maintains a dashboard including all pediatric COVID-19 cases requiring ICU care in North America. While it's not perfect ie. A case may be missed if not submitted or a pediatric death may not be captured if it occurs outside of an ICU, it's a great resource.

Emily Oster's newsletter Parent Data has great information for parents at interpreting the data and what it means for families.

RESOURCES FOR MENTAL HEALTH ISSUES

National Alliance on Mental Illness - their website has a lot of resources as well as a national hotline to help you find resources. The NAMI HelpLine can be reached Monday through Friday, 10 am–6 pm, ET. 1-800-950-NAMI (6264) or info@nami.org

Substance abuse and Mental Health Services Administration is a government agency that also provides a National Helpline, 1-800-662-HELP (4357) that provides confidential, free, 24-hour-a-day, 365-day-a-year, information, assistance and referrals, in English and Spanish, for people facing mental or substance use disorders.

National Suicide Prevention lifeline is open 24 hours 7 days a week to provide support in a crisis at 1-800-273-8255.

The National Domestic Violence hotline can help support survivors. Call 1–800–799–SAFE(7233) for a national 24/7 hotline.

The Child Mind Institute has an incredible website with resources for families looking to decide if their child needs mental health services or to learn about specific conditions. They also have tele-health resources available.

Florida State maintains an awesome website about helping children cope with toxic stress.

If you are a physician in the US struggling to cope during the pandemic, psychiatrists have put together a free and confidential helpline 8a-1a, 7 days a week. 1 (888) 409-0141.

RESOURCES ABOUT ANXIETY

3-6 year-old
Ruby finds a worry by Tom Percival
Wemberley Worried by Kevin Henkes
Scaredy Squirrel by Melanie Watt
Help your Dragon Deal with Anxiety by Steve Herman
Jabari Jumps by Gaia Cornwall

6-12 year old
What to do when you worry too much by Dawn Huebner
Guts by Raina Telgemeier
Sitting still like a frog: Mindfulness Exercises for Kids (and their Parents) by Eline Snel

Teens
The anxiety survival guide for Teens by Jennifer Shannon
Anxiety Sucks: A teen survival guide by Natasha Daniels
Mindfulness for Teens in 10 minutes a day: Exercises to feel calm, stay focused & be your best self by Jennie Marie Battistin

All ages
The Florida State University Center for Child Stress and Health has a ton of great resources for kids and parents.

Adults
Get out of your head: Stopping the spiral of toxic thoughts by Jennie Allen
Daring Greatly: How the courage to be vulnerable transforms the way we live, love, parent and lead by Brene Brown. I've heard her podcast is excellent.
Weight loss for busy physicians with Katrina Ubell MD while this podcast title may mislead you, I think everyone can benefit from Dr. Ubell's insights on how to handle stress.

BOOKS FOR YOUNG KIDS ABOUT CORONAVIRUS

A compilation of coronavirus books in multiple languages from the NYC Department of Education is available.

A hero too - by Lara Villani and Christina Rosato. A free e-book to benefit Save the Children.

Coronavirus - a book for children by Elizabeth Jenner, Kate Wilson & Nia Roberts. Illustrated by Axel Scheffler of the Gruffalo. Free.

Charlotte the scientist finds a cure - by Camille Andros - this sweet book is not specifically about coronavirus, but follows a bunny helping tackle a public health challenge.

BOOKS FOR KIDS TO ENCOURAGE SOCIAL SKILLS

3-7 year old
Have you filled a bucket today? by Carol McCloud
The Invisible string by Patrice Karst
Ladybug Girl and the Best Ever Playdate by David Soman and Jackie Davis (We love this whole series)
Chrysanthemum by Kevin Henkes
What should Danny do? Or *What should Darla do?* By Ganit & Adir Levy.
Should I share my ice cream? By Mo Willems

7-10 year old
The big life journal for kids
Auggie & Me: Three Wonder Stories by RJ Palacio

Teens
Social Media Workbook for Teens by Goali Saedi Bocci
Relationship Skills 101 for Teens: Your guide to dealing with difficult drama, stress and difficult emotions using DBT by Sheri Van Dijk

ACTIVITIES TO KEEP YOUNG KIDS BUSY AT HOME

Toddlers (2-6)

Busy toddler @busytoddler - Susie Allison former K & 1 teacher and mom has created an amazing resource with tons of resources for keeping children busy at home. Her "Playing Preschool" guide helped me keep my 2.5 year old engaged during lockdown.

Days with Grey @dayswithgrey - Beth is an educator and mom also has amazing resources including breakfast invitations. These are slightly easier to implement than an entire preschool curriculum. The idea is with a minute or two of planning that you start your family's day off screen free with easy fun activities for your kids so you can enjoy your coffee. Definitely worth checking out.

Oh Creative Day @ohcreativeday - Another favorite of mine, Shannon's resource is amazing at combining books with arts and crafts. If you are looking to inspire your little creators, check out the many ideas she has shared on instagram and her blog.

Counting with kids @countingwithkids - Neily a math education specialist shares play based activities to encourage early math skills.

Little Problem Solvers @littleproblemsolvers - Emily shares beautiful and simple STEM activities for preschoolers.

Preschool age 4-7

If you have little ones Pre-K to 1st grade, this website will offer a song and 2 read aloud books per day.

For math stories and activities Bedtime Math and Greg Tang are favorites.

RESOURCES TO HELP WITH SCHOOLING AT HOME

If you are considering schooling at home, your first resource should be your child's teacher who can make recommendations consistent with their level and curriculum. Local libraries often have a lot of free resources to support homeschooling such as Rosetta Stone. Here are some other places to start.

Wide open school by Common Sense Media. This website has a wealth of information about ways to help learners of all ages.

Khan academy - tons of free resources for preschool through grade 12. Sample curriculums and daily sample schedules for every age.

Outschool - Kids can take small group live courses with instructors on topics from learning to do a split and decorate a cupcake to high school biology and Python. For a cost, limited financial assistance.

Writing - Bestselling children's book author Kwame Alexander has free resources on his website including videos about how to write a poem.

Nasa – Free resources to teach children K-12 about STEM are available.

If you are planning to fully homeschool consider checking out:
- Reviews of various curriculums from Cathy Duffy available.
- A facebook group called "Secular academic and eclectic homeschool"
- Resources compiled by the Home School Legal Defense Association.

FAVORITE PARENTING BOOKS

If you're struggling with your baby or toddler's sleep one of my favorites is Dr. Marc Weissbluth's *Healthy Sleep Healthy Child.*

Another sleep book particularly helpful for helping train slightly older kids is *It's Never to late to sleep train* by Dr. Craig Canapri.

If you're struggling with tantrums, my go-to resource is *1, 2, 3 Magic* by Thomas Phelan PhD.

For kids slightly past tantrum age and hoping to improve your parenting, check out *How to talk so Kids will listen* by Adele Faber & Elaine Mazlish.

For food battles, Ellyn Satter's *How to get your Kid to eat but not too much* is a useful classic.

For helping your children through anxiety consider *Helping Your Anxious Child: A Step-by-Step Guide for Parents* by Ronald Rapee PhD.

Secrets of Happy Families by Bruce Feiler explores strategies such as family meetings and developing a family mission statement to promote happiness and teamwork in your home.

Common Sense Media has top-rate information about media use in children, as well as great lists of references and apps.

If you have no time to read more books, just follow me on instagram, I try to touch on all sorts of topics.

References

The following reference hyperlinks don't work in a paperback book, but if you're interested in reading more head to http://adviceigivemyfriends.com/paperback .

[1] Read more about toxic stress and adverse childhood experiences here.

[2] Siegel JD, Rhinehart E, Jackson M et al. CDC 2007 Guideline for isolation precautions: preventing transmission of infectious agents in healthcare settings.

[3] Stadnytskyi V, Bax C, Bax A, & Anfinrud P. "The airborne lifetime of small speech droplets and their potential importance in SARS-CoV-2 transmission." *PNAS* June 2, 2020 117(22) 11875-7.

[4] Schroeder I. "Covid-19: A risk assessment perspective" *J Chem Health Saf.* 2020 May.

[5] The pediatric data is extrapolated from the following correspondence that summarizes the results from Italy, the US, and 2 reports from China. The Coronavirus Infection in Pediatric Emergency Departments (CONFIDENCE) Research Group, "Children with COVID-19 in Pediatric Emergency Departments in Italy" New England Journal of Medicine, 2020; 383:187-190. The myalgias and loss of taste of smell data points are from the

reference below.

[6]The adult data here is taken from a large cohort of patients analyzed by the CDC and published in this report. Stokes EK, Zambrano LD, Anderson KN et al. "Coronavirus Disease 2019 Case Surveillance — United States, January 22-May 30, 2020." MMWR Morb Mortal Wkly Rep. 2020 Jun 19; 69 (24):759-765.

[7] Data derived from Kucirka LM, Lauer SA, Laeyendecker et al. "Variation in False-Negative Rate of RT-PCR-based SARS-CoV-2 Tests by time since Exposure." *Annals of Internal Medicine.* 13 May 2020.

[8] Long, Q., Tang, X., Shi, Q. *et al.* "Clinical and immunological assessment of asymptomatic SARS-CoV-2 infections." *Nat Med* (2020).

[9] CDC. "Flu Vaccination Coverage: United States 2018-2019."

[10] This number comes from the Lombardy region of Italy, where researchers completed contact tracing and examined close contacts of infected individuals and found 2,824 cases, only 31% of which mounted symptoms. Among people under 18, only 18% experienced symptoms. This article is not peer-reviewed.

[11] Read more about the impressive ways CHAM adapted during the coronavirus in this article. Philips K, Hong A, Buckenmyer T et al. "Rapid implementation of an Adult Coronavirus Disease 2019 Unit in a Children's Hospital." *Journal of Pediatrics*, July 2020; 222:22-27.

[12] CDC Covid-19 Response Team. "Coronavirus Disease 2019 in Children — United States February 12- April 2 2020". Morbidity and Mortality Weekly Report. April 2020 Volume 69(14): 422-426. It's worth noting that other smaller case series have reported lower numbers here, but I don't have enough information on the varying definitions of "underlying conditions" to give much more information.

[13] Similar numbers from multiple series including Wu Q, Xing Y, Shi L et al. "Coinfection and other clinical characteristics of COVID-19 in children." *Pediatrics* Jul 2020 146(1).

[14] CDC "Commercial Laboratory Seroprevalence Survey Data." Updated as of 6/26/20.

[15] Pathak EB, Salemi JL, Sobers N et al. "COVID-19 in children

in the United States: Intensive care admissions, estimated total infected, and projected numbers of severe pediatric cases in 2020." Journal of Public Health Management & Practice: July/August 2020: 26(5):325-333.

[16] Bellino S, Punzo O, Rota MC, et al. "COVID-19 disease severity risk factors for pediatric patients in Italy." *Pediatrics.* 2020.

[17] Clinical criteria from the CDC.

[18] Percentages are taken from two case series. 99 patients collected by NYSDOH published in: Dufort EM, Koumans EH, Chow EJ et al. "Multisystem Inflammatory Syndrome in Children in New York State." *New England Journal of Medicine.* June 29 2020. and 186 from a national sample published in: Feldstein LR, Rose EB, Horwitz JP et al. "Multisystem Inflammatory syndrome in U.S. Children and Adolescents." *New England Journal of Medicine.* June 29, 2020.

[19] Tenforde MW, Kim SS, Lindsell CJ, et al. Symptom Duration and Risk Factors for Delayed Return to Usual Health Among Outpatients with COVID-19 in a Multistate Health Care Systems Network — United States, March–June 2020. MMWR Morb Mortal Wkly Rep 2020;69:993-998.

[20] Carfi A, Bernabei R, & Landi F. Research letter: Persistent symptoms in patients after acute COVID-19. *JAMA.* 2020; 324(6):603-605. Doi:10.1001/jama2020.12603

[21] Lu Y, li X, Geng D et al. Cerebral micro-structural changes in COVID-19 patients - an MRI-based 3-month follow up study. *EClinical Medicine* (2020).

[22] CDC "Who is at risk for Severe Illness?."

[23] Boulad F, Kamboj M, Bouvier N et al. "Research letter: COVID-19 in children with cancer in New York City" *Jama Oncology,* Published online May 13, 2020. Gampel B, Lucas A, Broglie L et al. "COVID-19 in New York City oncology patients." *Pediatric Blood Cancer. 2020;* e28420.

[24] Shekerdemian LS, Mahmood NR, Wolfe KK et al. "Characteristics and outcomes of Children with COVID-19 infection admitted to U.S. and Canadian Intensive Care Units." *Jama Pediatrics.*

[25] Kainth MK, Goenka PK, Williamson KA et al. "Early experience of COVID-19 in a U.S. Children's Hospital." *Pediatrics*. 2020.

[26] Kelly Mom is an excellent resource for mother's struggling with lactation.

[27] Kainth MK, Goenka PK, Williamson KA et al. "Early experience of COVID-19 in a U.S. Children's Hospital." *Pediatrics*. 2020.

[28] CDC. Data and statistics on children's mental health.

[29] Meyerowitz-Katz G & Merone L. "A systematic review and meta-analysis of published research data on COVID-19 infection fatality rates." Pre-publication and has not been peer-reviewed.

[30] Covid Data Tracker under Demographic Trends of COVID-19 cases and deaths in the U.S. reported to the CDC.

[31] Perez-Saez J, Lauer S, Kaiser L et al. "Serology-informed estimates of SARS-COV-2 infection fatality risk in Geneva, Switzerland." Pre-publication data has NOT been peer-reviewed.

[32] This tool synthesizes geographic case data and individual risk factors to give you ballpark, specific information based on recent research.

[33] Dubin M. "'I am going to physically explode 'Mom rage in a pandemic" *The New York Times*, July 6, 2020

[34] Linder JA. "Don't Visit your Doctor in the Afternoon." *The New York Times* May 15 2019.

[35] Lakshmin P. "Mothers don't have to be martyrs." *The New York Times*. 5/5/20. Dr. Lakshmin is a powerful advocate for women's mental health and shares great advice on social media and her website.

[36] Ellington S, Strid P, Tong VT, et al. "Characteristics of Women of Reproductive Age with Laboratory-Confirmed SARS-CoV-2 Infection by Pregnancy Status — United States, January 22–June 7, 2020." MMWR Morb Mortal Wkly Rep 2020;69:769–775.

[37] Sutton D, Fuchs K, D'Alton M et al. "Universal screening for SARS-CoV-2 in Women Admitted for Delivery". N Engl J Med 2020; 382:2163-2164.

[38] American College of Obstetrics & Gynecology. Novel

Coronavirus — Key Updates (July 1, 2020).

[39] American College of Obstetrics & Gynecology — Committee on Obstetrics. "Influenza vaccination during pregnancy." Obstet Gynecol. 2018 Apr;131(4):e109-e114.

[40] 12% vs. 19.9% Lardieri A. "Cuomo: New York health care workers have lower infection rates from COVID-19." U.S. News & World Report May 7 2020.

[41] The chart was developed by consensus opinion.

[42] This actually happened on a JetBlue flight early in the pandemic. Mervosh S. "JetBlue bars passenger who flew with coronavirus" March 12, 2020.

[43] Carey B & Glanz J. "Travel from New York City Seeded Wave of U.S. Outbreaks." New York Times. Updated July 16, 2020.

[44] MGH has published an outstanding summary of the published literature regarding children and their risk of disease and transmission.

[45] Australian National Center for Immunization Research and Surveillance "COVID-19 in Schools – the Experience in NSW." 4/26/20.

[46] Park YJ, Choe YJ, Park O, Park SY, Kim YM, Kim J, et al. "Contact tracing during coronavirus disease outbreak, South Korea, 2020." Emerg Infect Dis. 2020 Oct [date cited].

[47] Goldstein D, Popescu A, & Hannah-Jones N. "As School Moves Online, Many Students Stay Logged out." and Oster E. "COVID-19, Learning Loss and Inequality." Published in ParentData newsletter.

[48] I got this number by assuming that 90% of children are asymptomatic, of the 10% who may be symptomatic, half may have a fever. It's a simplistic way to think about it, but still helpful.

[49] Allen J. "Schools for health: Risk reduction strategies for reopening schools."

[50] More details about what happened in Westchester and at the Choir Practice.

[51] Faden R, Faxon E, Anderon A et al. "The Ethics of K-12 School Reopening: Identifying and Addressing the Values at Stake." June 2020.

[52] Park YJ, Choe YJ, Park O, Park SY, Kim YM, Kim J, et al. "Contact tracing during coronavirus disease outbreak, South Korea, 2020." Emerg Infect Dis. 2020 Oct [date cited].

[53] Robertson N, Morrissey A, & Rouse E. "Play-based learning can set your child up for success at school and beyond". *The Conversation* 2/21/2018.

[54] Illinois State Board of Education. "Remote learning recommendations during COVID-19 Emergency" March 27, 2020.

[55] Zizenman N. "Can masks save us from more lockdowns? Here's what the science says." NPR July 23, 2020.

[56] 12% vs. 19.9% Lardieri A. "Cuomo: New York health care workers have lower infection rates from COVID-19." U. S. News & World Report May 7 2020.

Made in the USA
Middletown, DE
30 August 2020

17630870R00102